365 Days
of Organizing

365 Days of Organizing

A little help every day to become organized

JESSICA DECKER

ISBN: 978-1-7356542-0-1 (paperback)

January 1—Begin

Begin your new year with an organized intention. And know that there will be hiccups along the way. You may have to change some of the ways you've been doing things in the past, like putting your clothes in the hamper instead of on the chair in the corner of your room. If you want to become organized this year, follow this book for daily tips. We will take one word a day to help you organize your home and your life. You can begin on any day, and if you get derailed in your organizing intentions, begin again the next day. Each year, month, and day is a new beginning. Don't let yourself get caught in your past life of clutter. Begin your organized journey now.

January 2—Motivation

If your resolution is to become organized this year, you're probably very motivated since it's only January 2nd. Use that motivation to start an organizing project, no matter how large or small. Motivation will propel you to action, and action gets things done. Once you've completed a project, you're even more motivated to move on to another project. That's a great thing about motivation; it really gets you going. When you see progress toward your organizing goals, you're motivated to accomplish them. Use that momentum of accomplishing a goal to keep you motivated toward even larger goals throughout the year.

January 3—Design

Design and organization go hand in hand. Design to your style for you and your family by choosing furnishings that match your lifestyle. If you have pets and kids, maybe a white couch isn't a wise design choice, but a gray one can offer a lighter fabric and also hide some dirt and stains. Include organizational features in your design, such as a desk with drawers or shelves to hold all your books. Repurpose some items you already have by refreshing them with a coat of paint or new upholstery. Develop mood boards of spaces you love to cultivate your design style. Make your mark on your home through design and organization.

January 4—Baking

Take any unexpected time, like a snow day, to tackle your to-do list and take on an organizing project. On snow days you're likely to bake, so organizing a baking station is an easy project. Assemble all bakeware together; recycle or donate duplicates and pans that have seen better days. Nest similar sizes together and similar materials—glassware together, metal pans together. Keep baking utensils in a drawer close to the baking dishes and store the bowls in the same cabinet or near the baking dishes. Cookie sheets fit neatly in the drawer under the stove or in a long, narrow cabinet. Now that your baking area is organized, you may feel more inclined to bring out your inner Betty Crocker.

January 5—Taxes

The earlier you start gathering tax documents, the better off you'll be as tax time nears. Sort receipts into deductible categories—business, travel, home, education, and so on—and total the amounts in each category. If you're doing this manually, put the receipts in an envelope and write the total and category on the envelope. Digitize receipts to avoid storing the hardcopy and to have easier access to the information. Keep personal taxes and backup for three years, but always check www.irs.gov for up-to-date information. If you don't have an accountant prepare your taxes, consult with one for an hour. An accountant trained in state and federal tax laws will inform you on deductions to claim and could save you more than the cost of the consult.

January 6—Facebook

You've heard enough about the negatives of Facebook, but I believe it can help you organize your life. I regularly use Facebook to sign up to other websites, which saves me time creating and tracking usernames and passwords. Friends' and family's birthdays are recorded on Facebook, so I can easily see whose birthday is coming up and send them a physical card or give them a phone call. Facebook Marketplace is where I sell or give away items and can view a person's profile to screen them for my safety. I subscribe to local news feeds as well. In addition to all this, I manage my business marketing and belong to several small business groups through Facebook. Facebook combines multiple areas of my life into one website.

January 7—Thoughtful

To be thoughtful is to have careful, reasoned thinking. Be thoughtful when planning out an organizing project and incorporate all parties' requirements and understand all the needs of a certain space. Take a few minutes to plan a project to avoid costly, time-consuming mistakes. Be thoughtful by writing a list of needs and wants to uncover project priorities. Measure the space in preparation for furniture or containers. If you're organizing after a move, unpack and live in the space for a few days before hanging pictures or finalizing furniture placement. Design and organize with intention, be thoughtful about your space, and order will follow.

January 8—Unpack

Unpacking after a move is daunting; you're in a new space surrounded by mountains of boxes and can't even find your kitchen utensils. Don't panic; just approach unpacking in a systematic way. As a professional move manager, this is how I tackle unpacking. Move the boxes to the correct room. Unpack the contents and break down and remove the boxes and packaging. Put items away where they belong and then further organize later. Once you're out of boxes, it's easier to unpack the items because you're not moving boxes out of the way.

January 9—Binder

There are many ways to use a three-ring binder to organize. Some of my favorites include organizing bill paying by using bill-tracker printables and a zip envelope to hold a checkbook, envelopes, and stamps. Keep track of owner's manuals by sliding the manuals into clear sleeves and using tabs to separate the manuals by room—all manuals for the kitchen are together, the baby's room, and so forth. Create a home maintenance binder with tabs for repairs, cleaning, warranties, and so on. Binders can also be used to organize kids' schoolwork, personal schedules, or house projects. Find a way to make a three-ring binder work for organizing your life.

January 10—Hooks

Clear mini removable hooks are great for organizing necklaces and keeping them tangle-free on a wall. Store purses or scarves on a towel rod with S hooks. This same idea can be used in the kitchen to hold pots and pans or utensils. Hang hooks in your entryway for outerwear and bags. Hooks on the inside of a kitchen cabinet can hold potholders. If you need extra space in the bathroom, hang a hook by the sink and store your hairdryer. Stick a hook on the outside of a food canister to easily have the scoop available when you need it. If you have a large family—or a large personal care routine—use hooks in the shower to hang additional shower caddies.

January 11—Cords

Until technology advances and we're completely wireless, cords are something we have to deal with—hiding them from sight and organizing them. Keep extra cords labeled and organized by winding them and slipping them into empty toilet paper tubes. The tube keeps the cord together, and it's easily labeled on the outside. To minimize cord clutter in an entertainment center, run excess cords along the back frame of the unit, holding them in place with binder clips mounted to the underside of the unit, and zip tie any excess together where the cord plugs into the outlet. Create a washi tape label for the cord where it connects to the outlet for easy identification. When cords are labeled and organized, they don't become a tangle of technology.

January 12—Baskets

Attractive baskets add decor while hiding, storing, and organizing items. A large basket on the floor can keep a shredder out of sight. Pull out the cord and plug it in when it's needed. Store throw blankets in an attractive basket near the couch. Instead of a large toy chest, use smaller baskets to separate and corral toys by type. Keep stuffed animals in one, blocks in another, and so on until toys are corralled and organized. Slip a plant into a basket—place a liner to catch water—for an instantly attractive upgrade. Wire baskets hung on a wall can hold incoming mail; use one basket for each person in the family. Find a basket that works for your decor and organizational needs.

January 13—Jars

Mason jar organizing and decor may be on its way out, but the concept of using jars to organize is here to stay. Decant food into airtight, uniform jars in the kitchen. Use them in the bathroom to contain small personal care items such as cotton balls or Q-tips. Put pens and pencils in an attractive jar, or store small office supplies such as paperclips, binder clips, and pushpins. Fill a jar with small beads and store makeup brushes upright to keep the bristles in pristine condition. A wide-mouthed jar can be used to hold muffin pan liners. Get crafty and clean out and reuse candle jars and pasta sauce jars, or purchase mason jars in bulk at a craft or food-supply store.

January 14—Clipboards

Think of clipboards beyond the doctor's office. Use clipboards to display your child's artwork and easily switch it out as new masterpieces come in. Clipboards can be used in place of a corkboard in the office to hold small papers. Clipboards in a command center can hold lists and create separate sections. A clipboard per family member or day of the week keeps items ultra organized. Tie a pen on the binder to easily check things off or write things down. Decorate your clipboard to create a personalized look.

January 15—Magnets

Think beyond fridge magnets for how to organize with magnets. In fact, covering your fridge with magnets is actually disorganized. Use only the side of the fridge to hold papers. A magnetic strip on the kitchen backsplash keeps knives off the counter but still easily accessible. Glue magnets to the back of makeup cases and place on a metal sheet in the bathroom, preferably on the inside of a medicine cabinet. Magnetic strips in the garage can also keep drill bits organized. Magnetic chalkboard paint can be painted in an area for kids' art or a command center. You can write on the area or place items in the space.

January 16—Games

If you're trying to store games in a closet but you're low on shelf space, use a fabric sweater organizer that hangs from a closet rod to create vertical shelving for board games. A clear over-the-door shoe organizer easily stores card games slipped into a shoe slot. Ziploc bags store small, loose game pieces or games that have lost their box. Place a few of these in a bin on a shelf to further keep them organized. If you don't have a closet to store games, stack games on a bookshelf, largest to smallest. Weed out games that are missing pieces, duplicate games, or games that your kids have outgrown.

January 17—Rewards Cards

Use a hole punch to create a small hole in the corner of a rewards card. String multiple cards together on a ring hook and keep the cards in your purse or in the car so they're always accessible when you're out shopping. Better yet, some stores allow you to use your phone number to access savings, and you don't even have to have your rewards card. In that case, toss the card and just use your phone number to stay even more streamlined. In addition, the app Key Ring can keep your rewards cards digitally.

January 18—Pots and Pans

Pots and pans are so bulky and never store very compact. When organizing your pots and pans, nest them inside each other; this way they will take up as little space as possible. Store pots and pans in a cabinet near the stove, so they're handy when you need them. If your cabinets are full, you may have the ability to hang pots and pans on an overhead rack above the stove or kitchen island. Use rods and S hooks—or pegboard—to hang pots and pans by their handles on a wall. Slide the lid over the pan's handle to keep it organized and with the pan.

January 19—Pegboard

Pegboard is great to organize utilitarian items in the garage, but you can also use it to store items in the kitchen or craft room. Julia Child used a pegboard in her kitchen to keep her pots and pans organized. In an office or craft room, a pegboard can hang vertical paper holders to store craft or office papers. Don't have a drawer in your desk? everything you'd put in a drawer can go vertical on a pegboard and be easily organized and at your fingertips. An entryway pegboard is endlessly customizable for your family's needs. Paint your pegboard the same color as your wall to seamlessly blend in with your decor. Or paint it a standout accent color. Bring the pegboard out of the garage and into the home for a generously spacious and customizable organizing solution.

January 20—Busy Binder

Kids get bored when you're out. It happens. And parents have to deal with it. Busy binders are a great alternative to an iPad when you're out and your little one gets fussy. Fill a three-ring binder with clear sheet protectors and slip in small games. Include crayons and markers in a zip pouch. Hole punch a coloring book and place it in your busy binder. The possibilities are endless to customize your busy binder for your little one. Find what you think will keep them occupied. Once filled, the busy binder is very portable and organized.

January 21—Ikea Hacks

We've all seen the Ikea hacks online where someone transforms an Ikea spice rack into a bookshelf or takes a modern piece of Ikea furniture and creates a midcentury modern nightstand. The quality of Ikea furniture has improved in recent years, and I recommend strolling through the store to see what you can repurpose. Here are a few of my favorite easy Ikea hacks: magazine holder fixed to cabinet inside holds aluminum foil and plastic wrap, kitchen island with drawers as tool bench, plastic bag holder as wrapping paper holder, and a shoe cabinet repurposed as a scrapbook paper holder. Think outside of the box and channel your inner do it yourself (DIY).

January 22—Heirlooms

Heirlooms are mementos from loved ones, special items to bestow upon future generations. But what do you do with your grandmother's dining room set, for example? You could ask relatives if they'd like it to stay in the family. If there are no takers and you can't part with it, change its look with a new paint job or upholstery. If you don't want the item, donate to charity. Even if the heirlooms are small and can easily store away, see if a relative would love to have them, so the items get use rather than collect dust. Deal with unwanted heirlooms by: (1) reaching out to relatives to see if they'd be interested in the item; (2) repurposing or refreshing the item for yourself; (3) donating the item to someone who will love and use it.

January 23—Anxiety

Decluttering and organizing can provoke a lot of anxiety. You're dealing with emotions related to the items and your space, not to mention the emotional pull items have over you. I talk my clients down from the edge and reduce their anxiety by letting them know that they're not alone in their feelings. You can feel overwhelmed and hopeless about ever getting organized. That's ok. Just remember, your room/home/office didn't get disorganized in one day, so it's not going to get organized in one day, but it will get organized if you work at it. Organizing can be anxiety producing because it gets worse before it gets better. Just remember, it's a process and there's always a light at the end of the tunnel.

January 24—Broken Windows Theory

The theory states, "Maintaining urban environments to prevent small crimes helps create an atmosphere of order, preventing more serious crimes." For example, if some litter accumulates on a sidewalk, soon more litter accumulates. According to the theory, eventually, people start leaving bags of refuse there or even breaking into cars. We can take that example and apply it to home clutter. If there are toys on the floor, you're more likely to let your shoes and coat stay out rather than putting them away. Eventually that can snowball into leaving mail to pile up on the counter and clean laundry to go unfolded in a corner. A little disorganization invites a lot of disorganization. Conversely, maintaining an organizing system eliminates clutter accumulation.

January 25—Antiques

Antiques, in their original form or repurposed or restored into something new can add variety to decor. Reupholster old fabric to bring new life to an item. Paint or stain wood furniture to match your decor. Switch out hardware or match existing hardware if any pieces are broken or missing. Some antique items can be repurposed. For example, place baskets in a pie safe to add extra storage to a room or replace the tin doors with glass to make an attractive bookcase. Antique crates can be hung on a wall as shelves, or an old sewing machine can be made into a dressing table.

January 26—Printables

Don't recreate the wheel when making a list or calendar or tracker. Go online and search for printables of common things such as expense tracker, habit tracker, grocery list, packing list, meal planner, or chore chart. Whatever you're looking to track, chances are someone has already created a printable. Save yourself time and mental energy and use the printable that's already out there. If the printables available aren't exactly what you need, use them as a template and customize based on your needs.

January 27—Arts and Crafts

Whether you're crafty or have kids who are, arts and crafts can overwhelm a household. Keep arts and crafts organized by separating by function—painting, sewing, collage—and further separate by type—paper, paintbrushes, pencils, thread. Once you've done that, you're ready to contain the items. Purchase containers that hold all similar items together. A horizontal paper organizer is a great way to keep colored paper organized and easily accessible. Place jars on a lazy Susan to store collage supplies, pencils, or paintbrushes. Create art caddies filled with project supplies. Make arts and crafts easily accessible but also contained and organized for easy cleanup.

January 28—Plants

Houseplants add beauty and purify the air but can easily become unsightly and add clutter if they're not maintained. Incorporate plants and their maintenance into your home by selecting varieties that match your gardening ability and indoor lighting. Some hardy plants include the snake plant, spider plant, or a jade plant. Check lighting and care requirements to see if a plant is a good fit, and incorporate plant maintenance into your routine. If you group plants together, take care that you don't overcrowd the space to where it looks like a cluttered jungle. Instead, spread plants throughout the home to bring the benefits of greenery to every room. Even fake plants add beauty and require only a little dusting once in a while.

January 29—Desk

A cluttered and disorganized desk makes it harder to concentrate, and you lose papers and other items among the clutter. Assign zones to your desk so you can easily refer to a zone when looking for certain things like office supplies or paperwork. Create an inbox and outbox for paperwork, or use a vertical file holder to keep multiple projects handy. Have files you regularly refer to at arm's reach. Use desk drawers to containerize items such as pens and other office supplies. Have adequate task lighting and a comfortable chair. An organized desk will make you more productive.

January 30—Bags

Every client I've ever had has what I like to call the "bag of bags." These are disposable bags and shopping bags you quickly grab when heading out the door. They're a necessary part of every household, but what's not necessary is how many bags people keep. Here's how to keep a handle on the bag of bags. Assemble all bags and sort similar bags together—plastic bags, reusable bags, paper bags. Recycle at least half the bags. Organize the remaining bags by using the largest bag of each type and placing all other similar bags inside it. Do the same for each type of bag. The largest contains all the rest. If all the rest won't fit into the largest, further eliminate until they will.

January 31—Timer

You may think you have a handle on time management, but if you're not using a timer, you can get lost in what you're doing and lose track of time. When online, use a browser timer like Google Chrome's Tabs Timer, which allows you to set a countdown timer where tabs are automatically closed. Using a timer also helps people with attention deficit disorder (ADD) stay focused and on track. By setting a time limit on a task and a timer to keep track, you're more focused because you have an end time. Try using a timer to map out how much time you spend on certain activities to schedule your day. Manage your time, so it doesn't manage you.

February 1—Sunk Costs

I'm pulling out another economics phrase for you: sunk cost, a cost already incurred that you can't recover. It's sunk. You're not ever getting it back. So stop holding onto that blazer you bought but never wore or power tool you had to have but never used. Sunk costs, though already sunk, can further bring you down. Don't let the weight of past bad decisions bring down your present—and your future. Learn from your mistakes with sunk costs and move on; don't let them drown you.

February 2—Lighting

You may think of lighting as design, but it's also important for organization. If you don't have the correct lighting at your desk, organizing and managing paperwork can be impossible. If there isn't adequate lighting around your house, dark corners or backs of closets become literal black holes of disorganization. Increase lighting by placing additional light fixtures around your home, such as floor lamps, ceiling lamps, table lamps, and sconces. Have an electrician install lighting in areas where there is none or where current lighting is inadequate. Areas that need additional lighting include closets, the basement, attic, and garage. See how beautiful your home can be when everything is illuminated.

February 3—Bath Toys

Keep these toys from taking over your bathroom, already the smallest room in your home, by limiting their number and storing them to dry as soon as bath time is over. Use a plastic, ventilated scoop that can suction to the tub wall to corral toys and allow them to dry. Have your child put their toys back in the container at the end of bath time to teach them organizational skills. Rubber ducky bath time warning: Mold can grow in the holes of plastic toys. Make sure to squeeze out all the water before storing. Sterilize the toys by boiling them or placing them in the dishwasher's top rack a few times a month. Keeping bath toys clean and organized will make bath time enjoyable for you and your children.

February 4—Batteries

Batteries contain corrosive elements that can leak out over time. Proper storage is important. Store batteries in a plastic container where their contacts—the tops and bottoms—don't touch other batteries, preferably in a special battery storage box. New batteries should be stored separately from batteries that have been used but still have life left. Group similar batteries—AAA, AA, or D—together so you can easily take stock of what you have. Batteries stored in cold temperatures retain their charge longer than those stored at room temperature. Keep your battery box in the freezer to prolong battery life, and bring batteries back to room temperature before using them.

February 5—Mugs

An easy gift idea, mugs can soon get out of control in a kitchen cabinet. Assemble all mugs together and recycle any broken ones. Donate mugs you don't like, perhaps the one that came filled with chocolate as a gift. Once you have your mug collection pared down, use a shelf riser in your cabinet to double the storage space for mugs. Nesting mugs on top of each other causes breakage, but a shelf riser gives additional space and keeps mugs safe, organized, and ready to use.

February 6—Stationery

Letter writing is a lost art, but people still have stationery that needs to be organized. Whereas holiday cards used to be purchased and filled out, now people send out photo holiday cards. To start organizing stationery, recycle any stationery that has yellowed or is missing its card or envelope. Donate cards you will never use.

Separate the remaining cards by type: birthday, holiday, get well, blank, and so forth. Place the categorized cards in a sectioned container. This container can be as simple as a shoebox with colored paper dividers to note new sections. Label the container's card sections for easy retrieval. Stock up on occasion cards, like Mother's Day or birthday cards, so you always have them on hand should you quickly need one.

February 7—Light Bulbs

Separate by type of bulb into general categories, which include traditional, downlight, candelabra, and globe. Next, separate by how *warm* or *cool* the colors appear. Colors can vary from ultrawarm to cool daylight. When replacing bulbs, stick with similar shades of warm or cool to maintain unity in the room. Once bulbs are separated by type and how warm/cool they are, separate by wattage. Keep light bulbs organized in clear plastic shoeboxes, padding loose bulbs with tissue paper. Organizing light bulbs may seem like a tedious, unnecessary task, but when you're looking to replace a bulb, it will only take one glance to pick the correct replacement.

February 8—Nightstand

A tidy nightstand can contribute to a better night's sleep. Start off with a nightstand that has drawers to hide items you store by the bed. Only have in your nightstand the items you need when you're in bed. Clear away trash and extraneous items. Also, limit the number of books or magazines you have on the nightstand to only the current ones you're reading. In the drawers, separate items by type. Use small containers to corral tiny items such as lip balm or lotion. See how much better you sleep when your nightstand is pared down and organized.

February 9—Stockpiling

Big-box stores where you buy in bulk push storage responsibilities onto the consumer. If space is limited, how much is storing bulk items costing you in real estate? Think of your house in terms of price per foot. Put another way, it can get pretty *expensive* to dedicate a shelf in the hall closet to bulk items. Think of what you could have access to if you weren't storing a year's worth of toilet paper. Unless you're stockpiling for an actual emergency, purchase items when you need them. A deal isn't a deal if it's going to clutter up your home.

February 10—Lazy Susan

Despite its name, a lazy Susan, or turntable, is a workhorse in the kitchen, laundry room, office, or anywhere else you can think to place one. Use a lazy Susan to easily access spices and sauces in the cupboard with the flip of a wrist. There is even a double-decker lazy Susan for spices that maximizes vertical cabinet space, doubling the storage potential. Use a lazy Susan to store and retrieve cleaning supplies under the sink. A sectional lazy Susan can keep small office or craft supplies organized. With so many uses, a lazy Susan is not lazy at all.

February 11—Periodicals

The easiest way to reduce periodical clutter is to unsubscribe. Cancel newspaper and magazine subscriptions and get off mailing lists. If you need the information, it's online. If you can't bear to part with a periodical, access it digitally. You'll be saving the planet, saving your home from clutter, and saving a little money as well because online options are generally cheaper than print options. If you get periodicals delivered, only keep the current issue. Chances are, if you haven't read the last issue when a new one arrives, you won't ever read it. Recycle old periodicals or give them to someone who will enjoy the information.

February 12—Pillows

Throw pillows contribute to pillow clutter. If you switch out throw pillows, reuse the inserts and just replace the cover. You'll eliminate having to store excess pillows. Beds are frequently styled with multiple pillows, some only for show. When you get into bed, those pillows come off, never to be slept on; remove excess pillows permanently. This will also save time in the morning when you make your bed. When a pillow has come to the end of its life, give it to your local animal shelter to use for the animals.

February 13—Socks

The easiest way to never lose a sock and eliminate mismatched socks is to have only one brand and type of sock per style. For example, all gym socks are white Hanes, and all work socks are black Fruit of the Loom. This way it doesn't matter which two socks you choose; as long as they're the same color, they'll match. If you can't go this minimalist, separate socks by type: work socks, workout socks, hose, no-show, boot socks, and so on. Roll or fold socks with their mates to keep them organized and ready for use. Use drawer dividers in the top dresser drawer to keep socks separated and organized. If you have mis-matched socks after matching pairs, toss them in the wash. If they come back with their mate, put them in the drawer. If not, throw them away. Also toss threadbare socks and those that have lost their elasticity.

February 14—Love
How do you know what possessions you love? Think of the things you'd be sorry to see go. Think of what you'd miss if it weren't around. Think of what you'd grab, other than family members and pets, if there was an emergency and you had to leave your home in a second. Those are the things you love. Everything else is utilitarian or can be gotten rid of. Try this test: look around the room you're in now. If you don't love something, does it serve a necessary function—like a paperclip holder or a vegetable peeler? If not, donate it to someone who would love it or find utility in it.

February 15—Reality
Each home's reality is different. Your home's organizing reality is different from that of your best friend's or your siblings. This is because each family operates differently.

Work within the framework of your family and understand your home's reality. Is it a reality that laundry gets folded as soon as it's done? If not, create a space where a clean load can sit until it's addressed. The reality of many homes is that they have a junk drawer, counters aren't always clear, and laundry waits to be folded. That's ok. Reality is not glossy magazine cover worthy, but reality is where we live. Organize for your reality and give up perfection.

February 16—Help

Ask for help organizing if you need it. Not everyone is an organizing genius, but we can all learn from those who are. Get organizing ideas through books like this one, websites like Pinterest, and friends and family. If you can't bear to tackle a project alone, hire a professional organizer to help. They will help you go through your items and develop systems to keep you better organized. A professional organizer helps disorganized people become organized, and they don't judge or lecture. Don't be afraid to reach out for help if you need it. What's hard for someone is easy for someone else. We all have our strengths and weaknesses, and organizing doesn't come naturally to everyone. It's ok to ask for help.

February 17—Tupperware

A Tupperware collection always seems to grow over time. And tops and bottoms separate, never to be reunited. Periodically review your Tupperware to reunite tops with bottoms. Create more space by nesting similar items together and storing the tops in one area, arranged small to large. Recycle Tupperware that is excessively stained or where plastic is coming off resulting from too many times in the microwave. Get rid of takeout containers; they may be useful, but chances are you have much better Tupperware in your pantry, and you'll always get more takeout containers. Rightsizing the Tupperware area creates a big visual impact on your kitchen and makes it easier to access items the next time you have leftovers to store.

February 18—Tetris

Organizing is like Tetris, moving things around to find the best fit. If you love Tetris, try arranging small containers to hold items in a junk drawer. Exercising your spatial reasoning muscle makes it easier to recognize usable space. Soon, you can eyeball a suitcase and know what will fit— and what won't. You can move things around to find the best arrangement for a suitcase's tight space. Give the odd shapes of cleaning supplies the Tetris treatment and group by categories, placing categories together in a plastic bin. Infrequently used supplies go in the back under the sink while frequently used supplies get stored in the front. You can Tetris nearly anything to be a little more organized and contained.

February 19—Relax

The saying goes, "A rolling stone gathers no moss," but I'm sure it gets very tired. Everyone needs time to relax and unwind. We're all doing so much and striving for perfection that we sometimes forget to relax and take time for ourselves and for our family. Constantly running around is not sustainable. Relax and take a break every once in a while. Just make sure that break isn't too long. When you do get back from a hiatus, focus on one thing at a time. Relax and know that slow and steady wins the race. Some progress is better than burning yourself out and not finishing your goals.

February 20—Journals

Journaling reduces stress and creates a memory of your past. When you fill up a journal, put it away on a bookshelf or store it in a memory box to look back on later. Or throw it away or burn it if just the process of journaling is all you're looking to accomplish. Online journals can do the same thing of reducing stress and creating a timeline of your life. And they take up less room. Just back up your digital journals and place them in a safe location for future reference.

February 21—Manuals

Owner's manuals are often kept but barely referred to. However, when the information is needed, you don't want to search high and low to find the manual. Keep household manuals in a three-ring binder with sheet protectors. Slip the manual into a sheet protector and organize them by category, alphabetically, or by room. Before organizing manuals, recycle any manuals where you don't have the item, don't need to know how the item works, or can easily look up the information online. Store CDs or any product key information in the plastic sheet protector with the manual to keep it handy and organized.

February 22—Pens and Pencils

Every household has more pens and pencils than can ever be used. But when you need one, you can never find one. Start organizing pens and pencils by assigning zones where they will be kept. These zones are easy to identify; any place where you regularly write notes will need pens and pencils. These are commonly the kitchen, by the front door, in a nightstand, and in the office. Toss anything that can't write, and only store a handful of pens and pencils in one area. Extras can go with office supplies. Avoid picking up promotional pens to keep your pen stash in check.

February 23—Office Supplies

Office supplies are useful, and it's always good to have extra. Just keep backup office supplies organized so they are handy but don't get out of hand. Organize office supplies in one location. In this location, store together by type: writing instruments, paper and paper pads, printer supplies, paperclips and binder clips, and pushpins. Contain small items like paperclips in small plastic containers that can live in a drawer. Keep writing utensils handy in a decorative container on the desk. Store paper and ink near the printer. Recycle used paper pads and bent printer paper. Toss broken pencils and dried up pens and markers. Toss bent paperclips. Donate extra office supplies to a local nonprofit or a teacher who can use them in the classroom.

February 24—Garden

Even though they're stored outside the house, garden supplies need organizing to stay tidy. Set aside a zone in the garage to house garden supplies. Decant a potting soil bag into a lidded bin and include a scoop to make it easy to pour into pots. Clean tools after use and hang them on a pegboard wall. Replace broken tools and donate extra tools. Small tools and gloves can be housed in a garden bag or in a drawer or other container. Nest empty pots inside each other to maximize space by reducing the footprint they inhabit. An organized gardening area ensures that everything you need to plant and sow is readily accessible.

February 25—Notifications

Notifications are supposed to make life easier, to remind us of things that are important. But too often, notifications become annoyances. These beeps and pings become so numerous that we often overlook them. And what's the point of a notification if it goes unnoticed? Reduce notification overload by unsubscribing from unnecessary notifications. Turn off email notifications, and only check your phone when you're ready to address emails. If it's important, people know how to get ahold of you. Weather, news, and stock notifications that pop up on your phone also distract from current tasks and overload you with information. Make notifications scarce so that when you do get a beep or ping, you know it's important.

February 26—Broken

The saying goes, "If it ain't broke, don't fix it." But what happens when something does break? We've become a throwaway society and are more apt to toss something broken than fix it. What I often see is that when something is broken, it sits in the house, hoping for someone to come along and fix it. Broken appliances, clothing to be mended, and shoes to be cobbled all clutter up homes and are useless unless fixed. If a broken item is worth repairing, get it fixed right away, so you can start using it again. If an item isn't worth fixing, get rid of it right away, so it doesn't clutter your home.

February 27—DVDs

Not too long ago, if you wanted to watch a movie, you had to have it on DVD. Now, nearly everything is available at the push of a button. Review your DVD collection and donate any that you'd never watch again and any that can easily be found online. For the remainder, remove them from their bulky cases and place the disc in a CD/DVD multi case holder (a Case Logic disc holder works nicely). This streamlines your DVD collection to a fraction of its original size and reduces clutter to only the movies you really enjoy and can't easily access online.

February 28—Expired

Keep your pantry free of expired food by semiannually checking expiration dates. Adopt the first in, first out inventory method to use oldest food first. When putting groceries away, place newer food behind older food already in the pantry. For example, if you're stocking up on canned corn but already have two cans in the pantry, place newer cans behind older cans and move older cans to the front to use first. Avoid buying items you already have by shopping your pantry before grocery shopping. Plan meals and write a grocery list to accommodate meal plans. If it's not yet expired, donate food you know your family won't eat to a food pantry. This way someone will eat it before it expires, and your pantry will be clutter-free.

March 1—Maybe

Eliminate "maybe" from your vocabulary. "Maybe" just delays another decision. Either say yes or say no to obligations right away. When you tell someone "maybe," that means that they can ask you again, which then prompts you to answer with the yes or no that should have been given first or delay the subject further with an "I'm not sure." Be concise, direct, and confident when you commit to, or abstain from, an obligation. But whatever you do, don't delay a decision with a maybe. Close the loop with a yes or a no.

March 2—Medication

Medication can be lifesaving, but it can also cause a lot of harm if not properly stored and disposed of. Research online or ask your pharmacist how to recycle or properly dispose of unused or expired medication. Never flush medication down the toilet; it goes into the water supply.

Prescription and over-the-counter medication have an expiration date. Check expiration dates regularly to ensure that your stock on hand is up to date when you need it. Organize medication by symptom—cold and flu, blood pressure, and so on—and store in a location out of heat fluctuations and away from sunlight. Most importantly, keep medication out of the reach of children on a high shelf or in a locked cabinet.

March 3—Cutting Boards

Cutting boards are bulky, and you're constantly taking them out to use. Keep a cutting board on the counter and eliminate the need to store a bulky board. To store extra cutting boards, lay flat to store in a drawer. Place the largest board or the most infrequently used board on the bottom and the smallest or most-frequently used board on top of the stack. Alternatively, you can stand them sideways in a cabinet. Recycle plastic cutting boards when the plastic starts to shave off the board. Clean and oil bamboo or wooden cutting boards once a month, more or less depending on use.

March 4—Candles

Candles are an easy way to create decor in any space. Store candles not in use in a cool location away from sunlight. If your candles are scented, store in airtight containers such as Ziploc bags or tins. Sort candles by type to keep them organized. Taper candles with taper candles, jar candles with jar candles, pillar candles with pillar candles. Store matches and other candle accessories with the candles. If you have the space, store candlesticks and candle holders with candles to keep similar items together. Toss candles that no longer light or that are used up. Donate candles or candle holders you no longer want.

March 5—Podcasts

While I generally don't recommend multitasking, I love to listen to podcasts and work on something else. Podcasts help me pass the time when I'm doing housework, yard work, commuting, or any other mindless task. Like listening to the radio or having the TV on in the background, podcasts are a way for me to catch up on news or other subjects that interest me or become engrossed in a story. Search for a podcast that matches your interests and see how much more enjoyable routine tasks are now that you're entertained. I highly recommend any podcast on organizing.

March 6—Expectations

Everyone has expectations of how organized their life is supposed to be, but make sure your expectations are realistic. Don't set expectations so high that you never reach them and give up. And don't set them so low that you easily reach them and stop trying. Let your household know your organizing expectations. Children should know what is expected of them, and healthy relationships are built on communication and expectations. If you expect that you're going to put your shoes and coat away as soon as you step in the front door, they're never left out. If you expect your family to clear the table after dinner, there are never dishes left out. Organizing expectations create the groundwork for organizing habits.

March 7—Refrigerator

Keep your refrigerator organized and reduce food spoilage by assigning zones. I recommend the following: condiments on the door (complimentary condiments grouped together), a shelf for beverages, a shelf for leftovers and prepared food, a small drawer for cheeses and deli meats, a large drawer for vegetables, and a large drawer for fruits. When your refrigerator is sectioned into zones, you know where items live. When you know where items live, you can easily grab them, and they won't get lost and expire. Before you grocery shop, review the refrigerator to see what you need to stock up on. Whether you cook a lot or order in most nights, everyone benefits from an organized refrigerator.

March 8—Relationships

Close friendships or intimate relationships take time and energy. Think about the relationships you have. Are there any relationships that are a drain to your psyche? If there are any relationships you'd like to cultivate—"If only I had more time"—start spending your finite time and resources on relationships that build you up. Let go of relationships that bring you down or don't bring you any enjoyment. Instead of trying to befriend everyone, focus on relationships that will nurture your soul.

March 9—Plan

Planning is an important part of organizing. It's how you reach your goals. Whether it's cleaning out your closet or buying a new home, a plan of action outlines what you'll do and specific tasks to undertake. Plans can be written out or all in your head. You can plan for years or plan on the fly. Don't execute any task without first developing a plan. This includes mundane tasks like grocery shopping. Plan your trip into your schedule, and plan the groceries you'll buy, so you don't end up wandering the aisles and coming home without necessary items. And remember, "If the plan doesn't work, change the plan but never the goal." Make a plan and work the steps to help you achieve your goal.

March 10—PDCA

Plan, do, check, act (PDCA) is a business term for improving processes that you can apply to your everyday life. Plan: Assess current processes that aren't working. Think about what an organized home looks like for your life and develop a plan to get your home to the organized finish. Do: Enact the plan. Check: Review your organized home, assessing the new systems and processes and determining if they make your life better. Act: Adjust any processes made that aren't an improvement. Not every organizational system put into place is perfect upon implementation. Some systems need tweaks based on your household and how you use things. PDCA lets you refine systems and processes as your needs change.

March 11—Appliances

Small appliances abound in a modern household. There's a gadget to help steam, chop, warm, or cool. Some appliances are necessary and useful; others are clutter and just plain useless. Appliances make great gifts. Who wouldn't want to give their loved one something to make their life easier? I'm sure you've seen an electric wine bottle opener. Sure, it's useful, but is it necessary? Free your counter space, drawers, and cabinets of useless appliances and claim that space for something really useful.

March 12—Chargers and Adapters

I'm convinced chargers and adapters multiply when left alone. Keep chargers and adapters organized and under control by assembling them all together; sorting by type—mini USB, cell phone chargers, camera chargers and adapters, and so on—assessing what you need and don't need; purging broken, multiples, or orphaned chargers and adapters; and organizing what's left into a clear bin labeled Chargers and Adapters. If you have a lot of chargers and adapters, you can further separate the types into gallon-sized Ziploc bags and label the bag by type. Only the ones you use daily should be out; the rest should be stored away for when you need them.

March 13—Planner

Many people have made the shift to an online planner, and those are great. But if you're returning to paper planners, or you never left them, there are countless options out there. Do some research to find your best planner. A good planner is one you will carry with you and write in. An empty or incomplete planner is ineffective. You may need to rewrite some events on a family command center calendar to let others know of events that impact them. Doodle in your planner, put stickers all over it, but most of all, keep it handy and keep it updated to stay on top of and organized in your schedule.

March 14—Cleaning Supplies

Keep cleaning supplies out of the reach of children. This supersedes any organizing of supplies. Use cabinet locks or place supplies on a high shelf out of a child's reach. Now that the warning is over, here's how to organize cleaning supplies. Separate by type and use a plastic cleaning caddy to corral frequently used supplies. Cleaning supplies can live under the kitchen sink or in the laundry room. Extra supplies and infrequent supplies can be stored at the back of the cleaning supply shelf. Keep all cleaning supplies in one place. The exception is single-use cleaning wipes, which can be kept in the bathroom and kitchen for easy cleanup between deep cleaning.

March 15—Errands

Group errands together to be more efficient and reduce gas used running around town. Order online to save yourself the trip to the store. Hire a delivery service to run errands for you. The company, TaskRabbit, is in many metropolitan cities. Taskers help with household tasks including delivery/shopping. When running errands, use time in the car to listen to podcasts or audiobooks. This extra multitasking time can take your mind off the task at hand and make shuttling children to and from afterschool activities and grocery shopping a more pleasant experience. Maximize your time by bundling errands together, outsourcing them entirely, or multitasking to make them more enjoyable.

March 16—Picture Frames

When I organize clients' photos, I almost always open a box of old framed photos. I tell them to keep the picture and the frame or just the picture, or just the frame. It's ok to donate picture frames. In fact, they're one thing I see most frequently at thrift stores. Chances are you've got some photo frames given as a gift but never used, purchased yourself but never put up, or took down because your decor changed. Sure, you can save some for future photos, but let the majority of those old frames go to new homes. Somebody's going to pick it up and want to put their photo in it.

March 17—Linens

Linens are very easy to organize. I recommend using white for a clean, minimalist decor and streamlined organization. When every bathroom uses a white towel, there are no mismatched towels. White sheets evoke the pristine cleanliness of a hotel. Accessorize with colors in paint or wallpaper but keep linens white. To keep the linen closet organized, store sheet sets together and label the shelf where they reside with the size of the bed (king, queen, etc.). Store towels folded neatly by size. Stack body towels together, hand towels with each other, and then washcloths in their own pile. Having a monochromatic color scheme and storing linens folded neatly on labeled shelves will give you an enviously organized linen closet.

March 18—Legos

Store dismantled Lego sets in their original box. Contain all the pieces together with their instructions in a Ziploc bag. Large sets can be contained in multiple Ziplocs and placed on a shelf for future use. If you don't know which set the Lego pieces came from, contain pieces by color. Slip instruction books in a sheet protector in a three-ring binder labeled Lego Instruction Booklets. There are various storage options for Legos; I prefer a rolling cabinet with shallow drawers to store pieces. If you're displaying Lego creations, use the vertical space and place the masterpieces on a shelf. No matter what organizational system you decide to use, make sure you put the Legos away at the end of a play session because the system is only good if you use it.

March 19—Wallet

Is your wallet overflowing with cards and receipts? Give it a clean out to make it easier to find what you need. According to Feng Shui, old receipts hold the energy of money going *out* of your wallet. So take those out and file them away—or toss. Store gift cards on an app like Gyft and business cards on an app like CamCard, so they're handy but not cluttering up your wallet. Once you've gone through everything in your wallet, place only the items you need back in. Separate the wallet into zones: one for credit cards, another for insurance cards and your license, and another for cards such as a club card or a library card. In the money holder section, place bills facing out, smallest denomination to largest.

March 20—Vases

If you're like me, you love fresh flowers. People send them to me on special occasions, and they are a wonderful present. But when the flowers wilt and are thrown away, an empty glass vase is left. And plain glass vases from the florist aren't very beautiful. Keep your vase collection stocked with only the nicest vases. Recycle any chipped or broken vases and donate ones you no longer like. Store vases together near serving ware or in a high cabinet. If your vases look dull, dissolve a tablet of denture cleaner and they will sparkle again.

March 21—Notes

Whether you write notes using pen and paper or are a digital notetaker, notes can clutter up your space. Make notes effective and easily referenced by writing them down in one place—for example, a singular notebook or app. If you work best using sticky notes, keep them together in one place, like on a pinboard in your office. Create categories for your notes so they don't get jumbled together. Notes for work should be separated from notes for home. Likewise, notes for personal growth are separate from notes for others. Notes can be reminders or inspiration but are not lists. Those are covered extensively elsewhere in this book as they offer their own organizational challenges.

March 22—Bar

Use these tips to organize your bar area. Store all alcohol together and similar kinds of alcohol together (likes with likes). If wine or liquor needs to be chilled, store a bottle in the fridge or freezer and backup bottles with the other alcohol. Mixers should also get stored with the alcohol. Though if it's a general mixer like soda or juice that is consumed during other occasions, store it with other similar beverages. Barware like shakers and glasses should be stored near the liquor. Contain small barware accessories like stirrers, wine glass charms, and bottle openers in an attractive container if they're out in the open or in a clear plastic container if they're behind closed doors. An organized bar will make bartending your next gathering effortless.

March 23—Homework

Keep students organized with systems to track incoming and outgoing homework assignments. Use a small wall calendar for each student, placed by their desk or in the family command center. Write due dates on the calendar, updating with new assignments. Separate each student's assignments by subject in a three-ring binder. At the front of the binder, place a folder with one side labeled "incoming homework" and the other side labeled "outgoing homework." Set aside time each day for homework as part of the household routine. This could be while dinner is cooking, before bed, or right after school. By creating routines and using a calendar to visually track assignments, there should never be the excuse, "The dog ate my homework."

March 24—Undergarments

You may never have thought to organize your undergarments but rather toss them in a drawer and pull out whatever is clean. However, creating order in your undergarment drawer is easy. Start by emptying the drawer and sorting similar items together. Assess what you have and toss anything that is uncomfortable, stained, or torn. Using drawer dividers or shallow bins, create different zones in the drawer based on the items. Bras should line up with cups facing out, never twisting the bands or cups. Bra accessories like band extenders or interchangeable straps can store at the back of the bras in a clear Ziploc bag or shallow tray. In the underwear zone, separate thongs from bikinis and fold underwear. Organize your foundation garments to give your wardrobe a strong foundation.

March 25—Cooking

Assign zones in your kitchen for cookware and food. Store canned goods together, boxed goods together, and spices and seasonings together. Have your utensil drawer and cookware near the stove. If you're an avid baker, have an area where you store baking accessories. Icing and decorating tips can get stored in a clear plastic bin in the baking area to keep them together. Keep squares of felt between nested pots and pans to help eliminate scratches. Store lids near the pots and pans so they're easy to grab with the pot or pan. Use the vertical space on the inside of cabinet doors to hang potholders. Setting up your kitchen with these zones or *activity centers* will help keep it organized and also will help when you're cooking.

March 26—China

If you're not using your fine china, sell it to free up space in your home. If you use it infrequently, here's how to store china in a safe, organized way. Pack with packing paper, not newspaper, which will stain the china. Use *a lot* of packing paper padding. I mean *a lot*. Store the china on its side, not flat. When sideways, the weight of each piece is not on top of each other. Label the contents on the outside of the box and include a list of items on the inside. Store in sturdy plastic bins, or if your china is very precious, invest in specific china storage options. But still remember to label everything with pattern name, maker, pieces, and number of pieces. Include a photo of the complete set. This inventory will save you from having to unwrap the contents in the future to know what you have.

March 27—Computer Programs

Back in the day, computer programs used to come on discs. Way, way, back in the day the discs were floppy discs.

Now, computer programs are downloaded over high-speed Internet, and there is no need to have a physical copy of a disc. So go ahead and toss computer programs that are outdated or that are already installed on your computer. Keep the key information if you need it, and know that whatever you need can more than likely be found online.

March 28—Hats

Switch hats out seasonally and store with seasonal clothes. Winter caps get stored with winter coats and outerwear in summer, and beach hats and sun caps get stored away in winter. Don't bend or fold straw hats; they are easily misshapen. Instead, wad up packing paper and place inside the hat to help it keep its shape. Ball caps can be nested against one another by folding the back in toward the front and store easily on a shelf or in a basket. Keep hats in the hall closet since you put them on before heading out and take them off when arriving home. If you don't have a hall closet, use hooks in the entryway, or have a coatrack with a shelf to hold a basket of hats. Assign each person in the family their own basket with outerwear to include hats.

March 29—Furniture

Furniture can be very functional and can help organize a space. A buffet server can hold entertaining dishes, candles, and vases. Use a bench with built-in baskets to hold shopping bags for easy access. Tall bookcases can line a wall and look like built-ins. Decorate with baskets on the bottom to hold toys or electronics and intersperse decorative items among the bookshelves. Use a coffee table with drawers to store magazines and remotes. Or have a fabric ottoman that opens up and stores family games. A tray on top can corral remotes and hold drinks. Find pieces that are both functional and beautiful and use the storage they offer to have necessities handy and organized.

March 30—Education

Kids come home with so much paperwork from school, and at the end of the year, they're sent home with all the paperwork and artwork they've had stored at school! At the end of the school year, go through that grade's paperwork with your child and have them select the papers and artwork that are most important to them. Place these works in a storage box, label with the child's name and school year, and place with memories. Bringing your school-age child into this process gives them ownership over their own items and teaches them good organizing practices of keeping only the best, most representative sample of their education.

March 31—Credit Cards

Organize your credit cards by assembling all credit cards together and sorting by store credit cards, bank cards, and major credit cards. Assess the cards you have and purge the cards you don't want by closing the accounts—just shredding the card doesn't take it off your credit report or close the card. Keep only the cards you use frequently in your wallet and store the infrequent cards in their file in your filing system. For example, Discover Card gets stored in the Discover folder under *credit cards* in your filing system. Separate the cards in your wallet by type: store cards, bank cards, and major credit cards. You may need to store more than one card in a slot, but if you have them arranged by type, you'll know in which slot they're located for easy access when you need them.

April 1—Junk Mail

Visit https://dmachoice.thedma.org/ to remove yourself from junk mail. Opt out of the ValPak mailers at https://www.valpak.com/coupons/show/mailinglistsuppression. Next, visit https://www.optoutprescreen.com/, and finally, opt out of receiving the Yellow Pages by visiting https://www.yellowpagesoptout.com/. You can also write "return to sender" on the envelope and stick it back in your mailbox to have it returned to the company. Be patient. Sometimes it takes several months before your name is removed from mailing lists and catalogs. But stopping junk mail from coming into the house reduces clutter when dealing with the mail.

April 2—Electronics

Electronics age almost as quickly as the milk in your refrigerator. Assemble all electronic items together to start organizing. Recycle any outdated and broken electronics. Once down to only the electronics you want, separate by type. Common categories include headphones and music players, A/V equipment, chargers and adapters, and extension cords. Keep electronics near where you use them, preferably by the television. Or if there's no room for an abundance of electronics, store them in a utility area since they are utilitarian items. I like to store in clear plastic bins, but if you're storing in a place where the bins will be seen, use attractive baskets or bins to hide the contents.

April 3—Folding

Folding clothes using the "filing system" method increases space in the drawer for whatever you've folded. Filing system folding is folding an item of clothing as you normally would, then folding in half or thirds and placing the item upright in the drawer, like you'd place a file in a filing cabinet. Any item of clothing can be folded this way. However, clothes with a slippery fabric, like workout wear or lingerie, need to fit snug in the drawer to avoid slipping down. When clothing is folded in the filing system method, it's easy to see every piece of clothing when you open the drawer.

April 4—Exercise Equipment

Assign a zone where exercise equipment will live, create a home for all the items, and containerize them to keep the space neat and clear. Use a vertical dumbbell stand to take up as little floor space as possible. Roll up and store yoga mats in a corner using an attractive tall basket when not in use and try to purchase equipment that can fold up and store away, like a treadmill whose deck flips up to clear floor space. Keep small items like bands, gloves, and a jump rope together in a container with handles. When you have a nice, organized space to work out, it's more likely that you will work out.

April 5—Detox

Sometimes, it's easiest to jump into organizing with a detox. Pick your vice, whether it's shopping or procrastination, or something else, and start with a detox of the bad habits. Ban extraneous shopping for a week. This will reduce the number of items coming in to your home. Instead, shop your closet by wearing the new with tags items hanging there. This shopping detox will help break that habit. If you find it starting to creep in again, go on another shopping detox. The same goes for procrastination. For a whole week, whenever the thought to procrastinate comes into your mind, tell yourself that you're on a procrastination detox and go do what you need to do. Detox from bad habits to let in good habits.

April 6—Knives

Early into our dating, my husband bought me a new set of knives. What I'd been using were old, mismatched, and dull knives I picked up piecemeal over the years. Donate old, worn-out knives and toss ones with broken handles or points. Or even if your backup set is still good but you've got something even better, donate it and let someone else make meals for their family with the knives. If you don't store knives in a butcher block on the counter, store them on a magnetic strip mounted on the kitchen backsplash near where you prepare food. Alternatively, keep them near your food preparation area using a knife organizer specifically designed to fit into a drawer.

April 7—Empty Bottles/Containers

Sure, empty bottles are useful, but if you're looking to declutter, recycle all of them. You will always be able to get another tin or jar very quickly. Don't stockpile these items. Use the space instead to store stackable glass food containers. This will save space and be easier to store leftovers in the refrigerator when containers are similar and stackable. Many people keep takeout containers because they stack and are compact, but these plastic containers are made so cheaply that the lids crack easily. In addition, you shouldn't microwave leftovers in those plastic containers because, according to a Harvard study, "Old, scratched, or cracked containers, or those that have been microwaved many times, may leach out more plasticizers."

April 8—Emergency Supplies

An emergency supply stash ready to go is important to have in today's climate. According to the Federal Emergency Management Agency, an emergency supply kit should include:

- Three days' supply of water, nonperishable food and manual can opener; cooler, disposable plates, and utensils; pet food and water; and medication
- Toilet paper and paper towels; blankets, pillows, and sleeping bags; extra clothes

- First aid kit, medications, copies of prescriptions, and other special medical items; and supplies for babies or older adults
- Important documents and records; phone numbers of family and friends; photo IDs, proof of residence, and cash
- Battery-operated radio, flashlight with batteries, and booster cables and tools
- Road maps and a travel plan

April 9—Emergency Plan

Every family needs an emergency preparedness plan, because natural disasters happen all too frequently. Earthquakes, fires, tornadoes, and hurricanes cause devastating loss of life and property. Visit https://emergency.cdc.gov to develop and communicate an emergency plan for your family. Choose an emergency contact and memorize their number. Select a place to meet should family members get separated. Know the best escape route out of your home. Learn how and when to turn off the water, gas, and electricity at your home's main shut-off locations. Know where your fire extinguisher is and teach every family member how to use it. Preparation is key to keeping safe in an emergency situation.

April 10—Bookcases

Bookcases are great ways to maximize vertical space and hold books, toys in bins, and decorative items. Styled bookcases with decor interspersed between the books create visual displays and hold home decor along with books but don't overwhelm the space like a bookcase full of books might. Create a built-in look by lining a whole wall with bookcases. This is especially useful if you have a large collection of books. For children's rooms, I like to style bookcases with bins of toys on the bottom, books on the next shelf, and books and decor on further shelves. When installing bookcases in a child's room, anchor the furniture to the wall to avoid tipping and potential injury.

April 11—Lidless

Lidless Tupperware is absolutely useless. Recycle all your lidless Tupperware. Organize your Tupperware by assembling it all together and matching lids. If there are any bottoms without tops or tops without bottoms, they need to go. While you're at it, purge lidless sippy cups, bottles, and water bottles from your kitchen. But some things are good lidless. A laundry hamper without a lid makes it easier to toss in dirty clothes and toy bins without lids make for easy cleanup and toy access.

April 12—Bras

It's very important to keep the girls supported. You can do that by organizing your bras and storing them nicely. Preserve cup shape by storing bras cup-to-cup, with the outside of one bra nesting inside another bra. Tuck the straps into the space between the cups. When you open your bra drawer, you will be able to see each and every bra you own. Never fold a bra with a molded cup; this causes the cups to become misshapen. You can fold unmolded bras, such as sports bras or lace bras or those without any padding. Keep similar bras together, that way, when you're looking for a lace bra or a push-up bra, you know exactly where to go. Sort by color within bra type as well, lighter colors up front and darker colors toward the back.

April 13—Wedding Dress

A wedding dress is worn once, but we hold onto it forever. Many of us don't know what to do with the dress once the wedding is over. Should we preserve it in a box or hang it in the back of the closet? What do you do with a wedding dress? You can donate the dress. The Angel Gown Program (www.nicuhelpinghands.org) makes tiny gowns for babies who never make it home from the hospital. There are other foundations that give your cherished dress a new life and give someone a chance to have a beautiful gown on their special day. High school drama departments may want your old dress as well. Give your wedding dress a second life and reclaim that space in your closet.

April 14—First Aid Kit

Every home should have a fully stocked first aid kit. This kit should include latex gloves, bandages of various sizes, antibiotic ointment, antiseptic wipes, aspirin, tweezers, tongue depressor, gauze pads and gauze roll, cold compress, and a thermometer. Check the contents twice a year, ideally when you change the clocks for daylight savings time, to ensure that your first aid kit is stocked and at the ready for any emergency.

April 15—Business Cards

If you don't digitize business cards, you'll need to organize them. First, trash any that you won't ever use. Then, sort by category—for example, household will have business cards for a plumber, roofer, and so forth. Just like the yellow pages, sort by category, rather than company name, because you may not remember the company name, but you will know you need a plumber and can find that card easily. Use a three-ring binder with clear business card divider sheets. Label the tabbed dividers by the categories you previously sorted. For uncategorized business cards, label them alphabetically.

April 16—Action Items

Action items are those items that are immediately actionable. They are things you must do quickly—or else consequences are incurred. Keep action items in a place where they're readily accessible to you and easily seen to act upon. Action items can live in the family command center, in a vertical file on a desk, or as the first file in your filing cabinet. Wherever action items live, make sure you're addressing them daily. Even if you don't act on them, daily review keeps these important items top of mind.

April 17—Built-Ins

Built-in furniture, like bookcases with lower cabinets, is a great way to increase storage in a room without making it feel cluttered. Commonly you see built-ins in the living room around a fireplace, in a home office, or in a mudroom. These are places where items accumulate and need to be stored away. If you don't have these storage areas, create a built-in look using bookcases, cabinet doors, and molding to transform a plain wall lacking in storage into a beautiful built-in with ample storage.

April 18—Command Strips and Hooks

Command strips are Velcro or tape strips that hang home decor. Command hooks have a hook that attaches to the strip. Their claim to fame is that the strips remove easily without damaging the wall, with no nails necessary. Over the years, 3M, the maker of Command products, has come out with various Command items. There are now removable towel bars, decorative hooks, outdoor hooks, and mini hooks. Use Command hooks to hang potholders from a hook on an interior kitchen cabinet door. Use the towel rod in the bathroom to free up counter space. Mount remotes to appliances using Velcro strips. There are as many uses for Command products as there are Command products.

April 19—Balance

On one end of the organization scale are people who come in, drop everything, and never put anything away. On the other end are the people who can't have a thing out of place, or it drives them nuts. Create balance in your home by keeping it orderly but not so tidy that people are afraid to touch anything. Pick up and create homes for items but understand that, on some days, your shoes and purse are not going to make it back to their home. An organized home can be a livable home, even with children, if there's balance. Not everything will be perfect all the time, but there is order in assigning zones, creating homes, and containerizing. Use organizational systems and habits to create that balance between order and chaos.

April 20—Under Sink

Pipes under the sink often get in the way of drawers, so the area under the sink is an open canvas. Create those drawers by measuring the space in front of and between the pipes and purchasing clear plastic drawers to fill the space. If you keep tall items under the sink, use a plastic tray or lazy Susan (turntable) to corral them. Cleaning supplies don't always have to live under the sink. If you need the room in your kitchen, put cleaning supplies in a laundry area and use the space under the sink to store small appliances or other items.

April 21—Water Bottles

Sort through your water bottle collection and recycle any that match these criteria: lidless water bottles, moldy water bottles, extensively scratched water bottles, too big or too small water bottles, or water bottles you don't care for. Pare your collection down to just the ones you use and like to use. Invest in new water bottles if you need to. Reviewing your water bottle collection every once in a while keeps it from getting out of hand. I like to store water bottles upright in a drawer. You can also organize them on a shelf using wine bottle holders, which will keep the bottles from rolling around and give easy access to each one.

April 22—Bullet Journal

Bullet journals seem intimidating but are some of the easiest ways to journal. All you need is a notebook full of blank pages and a pen. Think of a bullet journal as a planner to keep you organized, one that you customize to your needs. A key and colors can help you visually see what's on your plate. What's great about a bullet journal is that it is up to you to record what you want to record, and you can write down anything, whether it's organizational projects, marathon training, or vacation planning. A bullet journal can keep you organized, but just like any system, it's only as good as the information you put into it.

April 23—Serving Ware

Serving ware isn't used every day, but it still needs to be stored for easy retrieval. Keep serving ware in the back of your silverware drawer because, essentially, serving ware is large silverware. Assess your serving ware needs and only keep on hand enough to set your table for a Thanksgiving dinner. This is generally a good standard for the largest meal you'd serve. For most people, a few large serving spoons and forks are enough to fulfill serving ware needs. Donate any extra and any mismatched sets. If the serving ware is silver, only polish before use and keep stored in protective silver bags.

April 24—Wrapping Paper

Keep rolls of wrapping paper stored upright or lying down to reduce tears and crimps in the paper. Use underbed bins to keep wrapping paper rolls contained. You can also store bows, ribbons, gift bags, and tissue paper in the box and hide it all away but yet keep it accessible. An alternative to under-the-bed storage is to store rolls of wrapping paper in a small, clean, round trashcan. No matter which way you store the rolls, slip a toilet paper roll cut lengthwise around the wrapping paper roll to keep it from unraveling. The toilet paper roll can easily be removed when you need to wrap a present.

April 25—Shower

The first step in organizing a shower is to remove all products from the shower. Toss any that are empty, nearly empty, and those you tried once but didn't like. Next, install a vertical shower caddy in the corner of the shower. Then, use the caddy shelves to separate products by person or by use. Only have one product per use. This means one shampoo, one conditioner, one body wash, one shaving cream, and so on. Bonus points are rewarded for a shampoo/conditioner combination to reduce a bottle. Hang any loofa or washcloths from the caddy and enjoy your next shower knowing you're not going to knock several bottles off the ledge when you reach for the soap.

April 26—Someday

Someday is a day that will never come, yet we hold onto items for a use *someday* in the future. Someday items are useful, which is why they're kept around. Someday items were purchased with good intent for a life you strive for.

Someday items can even be garbage, like empty boxes we hold onto because you never know when you need a good box. Someday items are even things that we may not care for, but someday, someone will. Donate someday items to someone who will use them today.

April 27—Cell Phones

Every few years, people replace their cell phones. And unless you trade in or recycle your old phone right there in the store, it usually sits in a drawer until it's joined in another few years by another cell phone. Some of these phones have photos or information you need to download, or some of them have SIM cards and information you need to destroy lest anyone get their hands on the phone. I'm here to tell you it's ok to let old cell phones go! Remove the information you need from the phone, remove the SIM card, and take the phone to any cellular retailer, and they will recycle it. Recycle the charger and any accessories while you're at it. Clear that space in your drawer for something useful and let cell phones of years past go to recycling.

April 28—Flyers

Whether you receive them in the mail, pick them up when running errands, or have them placed on your car or doorknob, flyers need not become permanent fixtures in your home. Read the information, decide whether you need to act on it, recycle it, or file it away for future reference. Don't let flyers become permanent residences of your countertops or car floorboards. Once the flyer is in your hand, like all paperwork, there are only three decisions: act on it, recycle it, or file it. Ninety-nine percent of the information on a flyer can be read and discarded.

April 29—Gift Bags and Boxes

Keep a supply of gift bags and boxes, along with wrapping paper and tissue paper, on hand to cover the last-minute gift-wrapping need. Store gift bags and gift boxes in a plastic tote or in an under-the-bed storage bin, along with other gift wrap necessities. While wrapping paper doesn't store well in a square box (see wrapping paper mentioned previously), you can store it with the gift wrap and boxes if it's in an under-the-bed bin. Separate your gift bags and boxes by category. Have all the birthday ones together, holiday ones together, and so on. Keep tissue paper separate since it can be used for multiple occasions. Make things easier on yourself by only using one color of tissue paper and, if you can, one type of bag.

April 30—Loans

Taking out a loan is a necessary part of living these days. Loans for things like a home, car, and school are beneficial to build a credit score, lending history, and help you achieve dreams of a stable home life and career. Keep on top of your loans by setting up automatic payments to ensure you don't miss a payment and damage your credit. Plus, when payments are automatic, they're built into your budget, and automatic payments make paying these large loans, well, automatic.

May 1—Hairbrushes

This may seem like a simple thing to organize, but many of my clients have hairbrushes that should be thrown away but instead hang out in the deep recesses under the bathroom sink or in the back of the linen closet. To organize hairbrushes, assemble all brushes and combs together. Sort likes with likes, and toss any that you don't use. This includes hairbrushes that are missing bristles, combs with broken teeth, and any hairbrushes or combs that you purchased but don't use. Once you're down to only the ones you use, clean them of any hair and place the ones you use daily with daily hair accessories. For all others, place with occasional hair accessories. Now getting ready in the morning will be a little less hair-raising.

May 2—Calendar

A calendar is one of the most powerful organizational tools available to you. Populate your calendar with obligations so you can visually see where you're supposed to be and when. You can also see your free time and where you're overextended. If your calendar isn't digital and needs input from multiple family members, keep the calendar in a central location, ideally the family command center. If your calendar is digital, send alerts to those invited to the event, so they can keep the information on their calendar as well. And remember, a calendar is only as good as the information put into it. Don't forget to write down appointments and events!

May 3—Greeting Cards

Keep greeting cards near present wrapping so you'll have a card ready when you give a gift. If you frequently use greeting cards without a gift, keep greeting cards with stationery. Where you store these depends on how you use them. Organizing *likes with likes* stores similar items together. Cards without a gift are stationery while cards with a gift are part of the present wrapping. Stock up on greeting cards so you always have some on hand should you have an occasion pop up.

May 4—Budget

If you don't track where your money goes, you won't know where your money goes. A budget is an important part of financial organization and responsibility. Know where you are spending your hard-earned money, and you can see ways to save or see if there are categories that are under or overestimated. Develop your monthly budget by recording recurring expenses with their actual amounts. For occasional expenses, take a quarterly snapshot of the expense and average the number to obtain a monthly budget amount. Review the budget to ensure that you're on track for your financial goals and tweak where necessary.

May 5—Glove Box

An organized car glove box should only hold information about the car, insurance paperwork, registration, the owner's manual, and any other car-related objects such as a tire pressure gauge, extra tire caps, and so forth. The glove box is your car's emergency information area. Keep it clear of clutter by storing pens, paper, tissues, mints, and anything else in the car's console. An organized glove box with the proper emergency information ensures that you're prepared should an emergency arise.

May 6—Home Binder

Keep a home binder with important numbers like the plumber, electrician, and any other service you use for your home. The home binder is also where you'd store warranties and owner's/instruction manuals. File information under separate tabs alphabetically by appliance or by room. For example, the kitchen tab would have the Samsung refrigerator, Kenmore dishwasher, Krups coffee maker, and so on. Remove old appliances as you add new owner's manuals and warranties. Make sure everyone in the household knows where the home binder is should they need to access the information.

May 7—Give Up

Don't give up on your organizational goals, or on any goals you truly want to accomplish. You don't have to start goals at the beginning of the year, week, or month. Goals can start over every day. However, there are some things you should give up, like self-doubt that you can never be an organized person. Give up procrastination, or at least don't make it a daily habit. Give up beating yourself up for not accomplishing your goals; remember that they can start again tomorrow. But never give up what's important to you.

May 8—Gratitude

Gratitude can go a long way in helping you to live a happy life. Be grateful for the things you can do, and don't dwell on the things you can't. Be grateful for what you have, like your home. No matter how cluttered it is, it's still your home, where you make memories and spend your time. When you approach disorganization and clutter with an air of gratitude for what the items have taught you or done for you over time, it's easier to see through the clutter to an organized future.

May 9—Skills

Every person I've ever met has a different skill set than the next. And things that come easy to one person, like orga-nizing, are difficult for another person to grasp. But this doesn't make the organized person any better or worse; they just have a different skill set. Be grateful for the skills you do have and rely on others to help you with the skill set you lack. You may do a skill share with a friend where you can help them in an area where they're weak, and they can help you in an area where you're weak. Skill-share groups are set up where people with various skills help each other. Who knows, maybe you'll even develop a new set of skills from someone who has a skill you'd like to learn.

May 10—Digitize

We're a digital world now, and that's not a bad thing. Keep your systems up to date and digitize important paperwork to have it readily available for yourself and others who may need it. Digitizing important documents like birth, death—including burial plots—and marriage records protects these documents from a fire, flood, or other natural disaster. You don't have to digitize everything, just the most important paperwork you wouldn't want to lose. Digitize the items that never expire, and you'll ensure that they'll always be available.

May 11—Craft Supplies

For children's craft supplies, store them in a handled caddy with divided sections. This way the whole caddy can move to the craft area when it's art time and can easily clear away when it's not. Keep only one type of craft in each craft caddy. Example categories include drawing and painting, stickers and free form art, or Play-Doh. In the divided sections, keep scissors, colored pencils and crayons, or pompom balls and glitter glue, depending on the type of craft caddy. Store coloring books and art paper in magazine holders that can easily be moved from a shelf to the crafting table. Organized crafts make for fun crafting, eliminating the need to search through a mountain of supplies.

May 12—Camping

To organize camping equipment, use large, clear plastic bins to categorize camping supplies. Organize backpacking supplies in one, tent and site supplies in another, food preparation supplies in another, and so on until you have your camping supplies categorized and containerized. Label these bins by writing with a large marker on an eight and a half by eleven sheet of paper and include a list of the bin's contents written on another sheet of paper and taped to the interior of the lid.

May 13—Sippy Cups

I have a toddler, and she has so many sippy cups. I don't know where they all come from. Organize sippy cups by first taking stock of what you have and recycling any topless or bottomless cups. Next, store lids and cups, and any other accessories like straws, together in a kitchen drawer, low enough that your toddler can grab them. Either put the lids with the cups as sets or put lids all in a container and cups in the drawer or on the shelf. By creating a zone, home, and container for sippy cups, you're ensuring that they have their own place to live and won't take over the adult cups and glasses shelf.

May 14—Envision

Envision your life organized. What does it look like? Take yourself from the moment you wake up to the moment you go to bed. Are you up on time or maybe a little earlier? Do you enter your bathroom to a clear countertop and then open an unstuffed closet to get dressed? Are you on time to your appointments, and is your car free from clutter? How does your home look when you envision an organized life? Use these thoughts to develop organizational goals. By envisioning where you want to be, you're motivated to do the steps required to get there.

May 15—Evaluate

Take stock of your current situation and evaluate where you can save time. Bundle errands together or say no to unnecessary obligations. By evaluating your schedule, you can see holes where you can fit in necessary items, or you'll see where you're double booked. By evaluating tasks at work, you may find things that are redundant or unnecessary, and by cutting those out, you can work smarter. Evaluate your home, work, and the way you manage your time. By evaluating your life and possessions, you're shining a spotlight on them, and you may see things differently. Ask yourself why you have certain items in your home, why you have certain things on your calendar, and why you do certain things at your job. Don't just go by the status quo. Evaluate.

May 16—Online Wallet

We always have our phone with us, and an online wallet makes it even easier to carry our wallet with us. Load credit cards onto your online wallet, which is connected to your phone, and thin out the cards you carry in your wallet, or leave it at home entirely. This way you'll always have a payment option at your fingertips. As an alternative even to an online wallet to pay for things, ditch cards altogether and use apps like PayPal, Venmo, Zelle, and a host of others.

May 17—Screws and Nails

I use a clear plastic multi drawer unit to organize and store my screws, nails, and other small hardware. Each category has its own separate drawer, and each drawer is labeled.

Finding a picture-hanging nail is easy now that they're separated from screws, wire, and other hardware. Further separate screws by size and type if you have a large collection. Store screws and nails near hammers and screwdrivers. This way you'll have the hardware and tools to complete a project.

May 18—Restock

Big-box stores and club stores want you to purchase in bulk, storing the items at your home rather than in their store. But don't let your home become a warehouse. Restock only when you're running low. Avoid the temptation to pick up something you use when it's on sale. The savings you'll gain today will be outweighed by the storage costs you'll incur by the purchase. Before you restock the refrigerator or pantry, take stock of what you have. You may end up finding an extra ketchup bottle or supply of paper towels you didn't know you had. Restock only when it's necessary, and restock only what's necessary.

May 19—Party Favors

The cheap, little toys and candy given as party favors seem to live inside their bags forever, forgotten and shoved aside or buried in the backseat of the car. Decline party favors if you can. If you must take a bag of party favors, pick out only the candy and toys that will be eaten and played with and toss the rest. There's no guilt in getting rid of party favors. If you're giving party favors and have leftover, incorporate the candy and toys into a prize jar that your children can choose from if they've earned a special treat.

May 20—Party Supplies

Themed parties are great fun, but what do you do with the themed supplies after the party? Chances are, you'll never use that theme again, but you'll keep the supplies on hand because they're usable. So use them. Pink polka dot paper plates can hold food just like any other paper plate, so can the mermaid themed cups. Use up leftover party supplies as you would any disposable tableware. It can even bring back that festive day to a boring, every day.

May 21—Accountability

Whatever you do, you don't have to do it alone. Studies show that having an accountability partner, someone who understands your goal and can hold you to it, helps you accomplish that goal. Whether it's organizing your home or writing a book, when you're accountable to someone, you're not alone. Regularly check in with your account ability partner and let them know how you're doing with your goal progress and where you're getting hung up. An accountability partner can offer suggestions or support to get you past your stumbling block. Accountability partners can be virtual or physical. You can even join a group and be accountable to the group. Whatever you do, don't go it alone.

May 22—Paperless

If you haven't gone paperless yet, now is the time, and here are the reasons why. Going paperless reduces your carbon footprint. Any information you need is easily accessible online, and it's accessible from anywhere. There is less paperwork to file when statements aren't lying around the house. Things can't get lost in the mail when they're delivered straight to your computer inbox. Going paperless can even mean refusing receipts or having them emailed rather than printed. If you use a credit card to make a purchase, most stores can look up the information with just a card—no receipt needed. Going paperless takes only seconds, and some companies even offer incentives to stop paper statements.

May 23—Outdoor Toys

Like with indoor toys, outdoor toys need a zone, a home, and in some cases a container. Set aside an area in the garage where a basket of balls can live and where bicycles are parked or hung from the ceiling to maximize vertical space. Make parking spaces for scooters and have hooks for helmets and safety gear. Chalk and bubbles can be contained in plastic bins, which are easy to cart outside during play. By assigning zones for outdoor toys, you create the space for them to live and know when they're out of place. Make it a habit for children to put their outdoor toys away, just like they would their indoor toys.

May 24—Samples

Samples are the little things we all take but most of us never use. Samples are useable, so we don't throw them away, but we also never use them. Sadly, samples end up sitting at the bottom of a drawer, cluttering our bathroom.

Tame your samples by using them when you get them or storing them to use for travel. If you end up storing samples, keep them all together in one place, so when you're packing, you go into your samples bin and take what you need. If you have many different types of samples—more than just shampoo, conditioner, and lotion—use small bags to separate sample categories. Containing samples to a bin makes them accessible and makes it more likely that you'll use them.

May 25—Repurpose

I love to repurpose things in unusual ways to aid in organizing. Apple product boxes make great desk drawer dividers. The bottom of an egg carton makes a handy paint tray for children. Foam pool noodles cut into fourths can be stuffed into tall boots to help them stay upright. Clean, empty candle jars make great containers for small items like buttons or bobby pins. A piece of driftwood can even be made into a jewelry holder. The possibilities for repurposing one thing into another thing to aid in organizing are endless.

May 26—Scarves

There are two types of scarves: decorative and winter. Store decorative scarves in your closet with clothes so you can pick out an outfit with the scarf. Store winter scarves in the hall closet so you can grab them when you're on your way out the door. I like to hang scarves on a scarf holder that looks like a hanger with holes in it where you poke the scarves through. For decorative scarves hung in a closet, I like to drape them over a horizontal bar where I can easily grab one to go with an outfit. Sort decorative scarves by color or material to keep them organized. This will also keep scarves from getting lost among each other.

May 27—One Hundred Things

Simplified down, the One Hundred Things Challenge is a way to live more simply with less. Owning only one hundred personal possessions is supposed to bring about a simpler, more meaningful life. These one hundred things don't include necessary household items like a can opener, but they could. The challenge is a personal challenge. Essentially, it asks: How much do we really need, and does our stuff make us happy? Would we be happy with less? Whether your list is one hundred things or more, evaluate everything you own, down to the number of pens in a drawer, and find your own possession happiness number.

May 28—Sheets

Have *a wear and a spare* sheet set for each bed in your home. One set on the bed, one set as a spare in the linen closet. Unless you're potty training young children, two sets of sheets are plenty. If you have an air mattress that you frequently use for guests, have two sets of sheets for that bed as well. The same count goes for pullout couches or futons. When one set is in the wash, the other is on the bed. Assess your sheet sets and donate to your local animal shelter any that are stained or missing pieces. Make sure every set of sheets has at least two pillowcases, or more if each person sleeps with more than one pillow. Fold sheet sets together and store in the linen closet or under the bed. Label the shelf or underbed storage container with the set size to keep them organized.

May 29—Deck/Patio/Porch

The weather is getting nicer, and you're spending more time on your deck, patio, or porch. Sweep off any leaf debris and dirt and wash any outdoor furniture that's been sitting over the winter. Dispose of broken or dead items, including pots and plants. Refresh pots with new flowers, refill bird feeders, and place cushions on furniture. To close down your deck/patio/porch in the fall, remove all fabric items, wash them, and place them in plastic bins in preparation for the spring. Empty out potted plants and stack the empty pots out of the way. Invest in a storage shed to store outdoor items or at least a storage bench that will offer some protection from the elements. Refresh your outdoor space in the spring and hibernate it in the fall.

May 30—Condiments

Fire up the grill and break out the condiments. And I don't mean the three half-used ketchups, watery mustard, or expired mayonnaise. Organize condiments before they take up permanent residence in your refrigerator and start to multiply. Store condiments on the door of the refrigerator and sort by type. Jelly and sweet items like syrup, for example, should be kept together while ketchup, mustard, and mayonnaise go in another section. Salad dressings are another category to keep together. Occasionally review expiration dates and replace bottles when they are nearly empty to avoid the splatter that happens when a condiment is at the end of the bottle.

May 31—Small Bags

I am in love with small bags to organize items. I use attractive zippered pouches in my purse to organize daily necessities. In the playroom I use clear pouches to hold loose games or game parts. Ziploc bags of snack, sandwich, quart, and gallon size help organize anything from food to toiletry samples. I keep a small, empty foldable bag in my purse in case I'm out shopping and need an extra bag. This small bag unfolds to be a large bag and is very handy. Small bags can help organize travel supplies or a purse for everyday travel around town. Though the bags are small, they're mighty useful.

June 1—Bathing Suits

Now that it's summer, pull out the bathing suits and get ready for the beach or pool! Keep bathing suits in their own drawer, along with any swim accessories like cover-ups, goggles, and swim caps. Store sets together and use drawer dividers to keep bathing suits separate from swim accessories. Bathing suits are slippery, but try to keep them upright in the drawer so you can see what you have. Wash your bathing suit after every swim and hang it to air dry. Toss any bathing suits with corroded elastic or slouchy straps. Unless you frequent a pool year-round, seasonal switch your bathing suit drawer with its winter counterpart, thermal wear.

June 2—Renew

You're halfway through the year. Your home and life should already be very organized. Renew and revive your organizational systems, revising what doesn't work any longer and refreshing the systems that still work for you. Renew your linen closet by donating old towels and blankets to your local animal shelter. When you take time to renew your system, you breathe life into your home. Renew your intention for the second half of the year and continue with your organizing progress.

June 3—File

There are only three decisions when it comes to paperwork. Act on it, trash it, or file it. File your paperwork weekly so it doesn't accumulate into a mountain of filing that you dread addressing and ultimately ignore. Before you start filing, separate the pile into categories to easily view and assess each category as a whole. A good filing system has a category and subcategory for the papers you need to store, keeps necessary papers easily retrievable, and keeps you on top of bills and other important documents.

June 4—Enough

How do you know when your home and your schedule have had enough? Don't wait until they're both bursting at the seams and you can't cram another pair of shoes into your closet or another activity into your day. Learn to say no before your schedule has had enough. When you say you've had enough, mean it. Learn to take items out of your cart, in store and online, before they become clutter in your home. When using containers to corral items, like socks or art supplies, fill it only to the top, not bursting at the seams. Once the container is filled, you have enough of an item. You have a finite amount of space in your home and time in your day, and once a space is filled or your day is booked, you have enough.

June 5—Closets

Keep your closets clutter-free by maintaining equilibrium. Only have as much in your closet as you have room for. Maximize space by using double-hanging rods. Hang shirts on the top rod, and hang pants and skirts on the bottom rod. Organize your closet by color and sleeve-length, sleeveless to long-sleeved, light colored to dark colored. Place shoes on shelves lined with a plastic liner, or on the bottom of the closet on an expandable shoe rack, or on the door in an over-the-door rack. An organized closet will make getting dressed in the morning something you look forward to.

June 6—KonMari

The KonMari Method is an established way to organize from Japanese organizing consultant Marie Kondo. Based in minimalism, KonMari teaches you keep only items that *spark joy*. Use this mantra to go through your closet and ask yourself, for every item, does it spark joy? Donate anything you're ambivalent about and anything that absolutely doesn't bring you joy. Move through every area of your home and repeat this exercise until you have nothing in your home that does not spark joy.

June 7—Kids' Rooms

Kids are constantly growing, and their rooms need an occasional review to ensure that their bedroom keeps pace. Organize age-appropriate books on a bookshelf in themes, fiction, nonfiction, history, or poetry. Create a cozy corner for reading. Clear off a desk for studying and provide good lighting and a comfortable, sturdy chair. In the closet and dressers, donate outgrown clothes. If you can, remove most of the toys and place them in the playroom to make the bedroom a haven of quiet reading, studying, and sleeping.

June 8—Label

There's nothing I like more than a good label. A good label will help maintain an organizational system. They let people know what belongs and what doesn't. Label the drawers in your dresser. Label the shelves in your kitchen. Label the manila folders in your filing system. Label the bins under your bathroom sink. Label everything.

June 9—Contain

Contain yourself and your possessions. Keep items from running amok in your home with a basket or bin. Use plastic, washable bins in the kitchen and bathroom. Large bins can hold large items like sports balls. Small bins can hold things like paperclips or bobby pins. The container you use must match the volume of what you're storing. Break items down into smaller categories. "Toys" should be separated and contained into "trucks," "trains," "dolls," "animals," and so forth. By containing items, you corral them and keep your home tidy.

June 10—Decor

Organizing your home sets the framework, but decorating your home really makes it a place to enjoy. Your decor should match your tastes, not the trend of the moment. Your home needs to function for your family, which may mean that toys live in the living room—organized in a corner in bins of course. Decor is the finishing touch on the masterpiece that is your home. If you're on a budget, shop at garage sales and online swap groups to find treasures that won't break the bank. Whether your style is modern, traditional, eclectic, or a mix of them all, find the decor that speaks to you.

June 11—Memorabilia

We all have memories that we store, and it's ok to keep these things. Remember the past, cherish it, and store a few memorabilia to remember the good times. Don't keep memorabilia that makes you sad, such as tokens from past relationships. If you're storing a lot of memorabilia, break it up by category: childhood, high school, college, wedding, vacations; or decade: 1990 – 2000. When storing your children's memorabilia, have a memory box for each child and add to it as they grow. Occasionally look through your memory box and weed out things that no longer hold meaning.

June 12—Photos

Store photos in an archival-quality album or archival-quality photo box and sort by category or date. You may also sort within the category or date as well. If you have a photo box labeled "vacation," you may subcategorize the vacations by years or by location. If you label an album by date, such as "2010," you can label the pages by category, such as "Thanksgiving" or "Grandma's Eightieth Birthday." Toss generic photos—we all know what a beach looks like—and send duplicate photos to friends or relatives who would enjoy the photo or who were at the event with you. By paring down your photos and grouping them, you create a record of the past that can be displayed and enjoyed.

June 13—Drawers

Keep the following clothing types in drawers: bras, underwear, socks, PJs, lounge clothing, and workout clothing. Organize drawers from the top down. Socks, underwear, and bras go in the top drawers followed by PJs and then lounge clothing, with workout clothing in the bottom drawer. A top drawer can be used as a valet area for jewelry or makeup. Use drawer dividers to section the drawers and keep socks and underwear corralled. Store bras cup to cup, and don't bend one cup into the other—this distorts the cup shape. Use the filing system method in drawers, turning shirts and pants vertical rather than lying horizontal. This allows you to see every piece of clothing rather than just the top shirt or pant. This general drawer organization is one I use most often when organizing and it works for most clothing situations.

June 14—Assemble

When you begin an organization project, assemble similar items together, likes with likes. This allows you to address everything in that category. If you're organizing your books, assemble *all* your books to review. Assembling items together allows you to see the volume of what you have and weed out any duplicates or things that have *seen better days*. You don't know how many black T-shirts you have unless you assemble them all together. You may be unwilling to part with something that's stained or torn if you think you don't have a replacement. Assembling similar items also lets you know the container size or storage space you need to hold everything. Assembling is the first step to organizing.

June 15—Assess

Once you've assembled similar items, assess them together. Donate duplicates or items that have *seen better days*. In a kitchen, you're bound to have multiple pans around the same size but all in different states of wear. Toss pans that are excessively scratched and use the newer ones that you may have forgotten about before you assembled and assessed your similar items. Assess your possessions with a critical eye. Ask yourself, "If I were shopping today, would I buy this?" If the answer is no, then donate the item to someone who would enjoy it. Assess and address things you've been putting off. If you have a pile of mail, sort it into categories, assemble similar items together, and assess what you need to act on, file, or trash.

June 16—Just Do It

If a task takes less than a minute, and you're not in the middle of another task, just do it. Don't put off until tomorrow what you can easily tackle today. Imagine the accomplishment you will feel when you just do it now rather than just do it later. Just do it later means you have to schedule a time, put it on your to-do list, and have it hanging over your head. Just do it now, and then it's done.

June 17—Laundry

The laundry pile can easily become a laundry mountain if you don't have a regular laundry system. Start your laundry system with a laundry basket in each bedroom. If a laundry basket lid stops clothes from making it into the basket, remove the lid. Make it as easy as possible for your family to put dirty clothes in the laundry basket. Next, once a day, or at least once a week, do the laundry. A friend of mine has a different laundry day for each family member and then one day for towels and sheets. This way she's not running to various rooms in the house putting away a single load of clothes. Separate dry cleaning from regular wash and send dry cleaning out on a schedule. Once you have a system, laundry becomes automatic and less of a dreaded chore.

June 18—Chores

When I was growing up, I had daily chores around the house. I would sweep, vacuum, empty or load the dishwasher, and make my bed. Assigning chores to your children teaches them accountability and responsibility. Tying in an allowance with chores builds a reward system and teaches children the value of money. There are numerous chore templates online. Find one that matches your family style and your child's responsibility level. It's never too early to teach children as young as two to pick up their toys when they're finished playing. Even if you have a housekeeper, children can still perform chores such as feeding, brushing, or walking the pets, and making their own bed.

June 19—Zone

Assign zones in your home so you know where things belong. Zones can be as large as your entryway to as small as a snack shelf. Zones set the tone for the space and name what does or does not live there. The entryway zone contains items you use outside the house, such as umbrellas, coats, and hats. It also includes a landing zone where you place things like your keys, change, and sunglasses. Once you know what lives in the zone, it's easy to spot things that don't belong. When items from one zone creep into another—for example, books on the kitchen counter—you move them to the zone where they belong. Zones make organization automatic, and by automating decisions you reduce the brainpower required to maintain an organized home.

June 20—Family Room

The family room is where your family gathers to watch TV and play games, and the kids usually have some toys here. This space, as the name implies, is all about the family. Organize this room for children and adults. Keep breakables away from little hands and furnish the room with easy-to-clean furniture. A storage ottoman can hold games and double as extra seating. Trays on the ottoman can hold drinks and snacks. Oversized pillows can be thrown on the floor to provide additional seating. A decorative box on the media console creates a home and a container for remotes. Baskets and bins attractively hold toys and provide easy accessibility. Make the family room a comfortable, organized, kid-friendly zone where the whole family can unwind.

June 21—Text Messages

Once sent and addressed, text messages can be deleted. Think of text messages as mini emails. The inbox is the message center, and only active messages are saved. Once a conversation is over, you can delete the message. If you still need to address something with that person, their message is undeleted in the message center, and is still current. This way, if you answer a text when you're unable to address it, you can refer to your message center when you're ready. Keep your text message center cleared out of old conversations, so it's easy to see what's current. With a more organized way of addressing messages, you can ensure that all messages are addressed.

June 22—Mail

The old saying, "No news is good news," is especially true with mail. Reduce the amount of mail you receive by signing up for online bill pay and paperless statements. When you check your mail, do it over the trash can, where you can toss junk mail without even opening it and read and toss any mail you don't need to act on or file. Unsubscribe from catalogs. By reducing the amount of mail in your mailbox and quickly making decisions about and eliminating mail you don't need, you can easily manage your mailbox. The same goes for your email inbox, unsubscribe from the unnecessary, read and delete, or leave the email in your inbox to address later.

June 23—Counters

Cluttered counters easily make your home look cluttered. Keep your counters clear by assigning a place for everything that resides on your countertops. Use a magnetic strip to store knives on the kitchen's backsplash. A junk drawer is useful to hold small items, like a pen and pad of paper, membership cards, and any other items that need to be easily accessible. Store away infrequently used appliances. Keep toiletries and your toothbrush in a drawer or medicine cabinet to clear off the bathroom counter. Be diligent about keeping your counters clear, and your home will look more organized because of it.

June 24—Order

Create order in your home and in your life. Order in one area will help create or maintain order in another. "When you live surrounded by clutter, it is impossible to have clarity about what you are doing in your life," says Karen Kingston. A home in order tends to stay in order with a little daily maintenance. Once there is a place for everything, an order to the home, everything can find its way to its place. Adding order to your life means managing your schedule and carving out *me time*. Order your life by making time for the things that are necessary and important to you. When you order your schedule, you feel more in control of your time. When you order your home, you feel happier about your surroundings.

June 25—Makeup

Did you know that makeup has an expiration date? Liquids last about six months while powders and lipsticks last about two years. Use expiration dates as a starting place to organize your makeup. Once you've tossed expired makeup, sort by categories and weed out makeup you no longer like. Now that you're down to the makeup that's not expired and that you enjoy wearing, store everyday makeup you take with you in a small travel makeup pouch. For makeup you store at home, keep it out of the bathroom where moisture and heat break down your makeup. Keep makeup in clear acrylic containers with compartments for lipstick and drawers for pencils and powders. Store occasional makeup by type in the linen closet. An organized makeup area eliminates the chances of an eyeliner getting lost in a sea of lip pencils and opening three bronzers before finally finding the blush compact you're searching for.

June 26—Consignment

Online consignment and resale are having a moment right now. What started more than twenty years ago with eBay has now grown to thredUP, Poshmark, The RealReal, and even Facebook Marketplace, to name a few of the sites and apps where you can send items in for resale or sell the items yourself. Make money off the items in your home and closet that you don't love. Items as obscure as novelty pins or electronics sell well on eBay while Poshmark focuses on clothing and accessories, and The RealReal sells mainly high-end clothing and accessories like Chanel and Louis Vuitton. Chances are, if you don't want it, there's someone online who does.

June 27—Everything

"A place for everything, and everything in its place." An organized home has assigned a place for everything, and everything is in its place. Address everything when you organize, not just items on the surface. Open cabinets and closets to uncover everything you're storing. Remember that you don't need to keep everything, you can let things go. Clear out everything in your storage unit and garage to see what's there, then create organizational systems for everything you put back. An organized home has everything in its right place, and everything is organized.

June 28—Garage

Use pegboard and hooks on the walls of your garage to maximize the vertical space. Store items in plastic bins to ward off the elements and creepy crawlies. Install shelving for the bins along the edge of the garage to keep the center clear for an automobile or easy access for projects. Install shelving above the garage door for even more storage for seasonal items. House gardening supplies near the garage door, making it easy to pull items like a lawnmower and weed trimmer in and out. Store kids' outdoor toys near the garage door so they can easily play with them. Draw parking spaces on the floor for children's bikes and scooters to keep them organized too. Now that your garage is organized, you can even park the car in there.

June 29—Personal Space

We all need a personal space to unwind; even children need their own corner of a shared room. When creating this space, think of what makes you happy, and design that into the space. Make sure your personal space is uncluttered. Flush out everything that doesn't belong in the space and anything that brings you down. If you're creating this space for a child, get their input into what makes them happy. Have them collect items to decorate their space. Let their creativity flow into the design of the space. Everyone's personal space is different and reflects their secret, sacred self.

June 30—Organization

Organization means something different to each person. There are different levels of organization a person desires in their life. Some people even desire more organization than they can achieve. Life events cause organizational levels to change. A family with little children has a different level of organization than a young college student. Find the level of organization you can achieve and easily maintain. Once you're organized, maintaining your organizational systems should become routine. Once they are routine, organization will become less painful. Sure, you still have to put things away, but when your home is organized, maintaining organization is a pleasure.

July 1—Excuses

No excuses. Banish organizing excuses like "I just can't get organized" and "I'm not an organized person." Anyone can become organized; you don't have to be born an organized person. Likewise, there's always a right time to organize. If you have young children who always pull out the toys you've just organized, that doesn't defeat your organization—it models organized behavior for your children. If you're too tired to organize, just do as much as you can; sorting and addressing mail requires minimal physical energy. Nothing is accomplished when you make excuses as to why you can't be organized or make excuses that stop you from organizing.

July 2—Donate

Do good and donate your used and unwanted goods. Someone is sure to see the items you no longer want or need and have a use for them. Send your old things to become someone's new things. Give them another life and donate them. Look online for your local Goodwill, Salvation Army, or another donation center. Some places will even pick up your donations. Donating unclutters your home and helps others in the process. Don't hesitate, donate!

July 3—Reframe

Take a step back and reframe the way you think about your home. If you were entering your home for the first time, what would you think about the way it looks? How can you improve the way things function? Are there items you would buy or items you would donate to make the home look better? Ask a neutral friend or family member to review your home. Review what's working and what's not working in your life and your home and reframe your thinking to uncover new ways to address organization and time-management challenges.

July 4—Independence

Declare independence from your clutter. Break free from whatever binds you to your stuff. Revolt against possessions that bring you down. In order to feel completely free from clutter, let it go. Allow yourself to live without it, independent of your need for unnecessary possessions. The easiest way to reduce clutter in your home is to not let it in your home in the first place. If you don't have it, you don't have to clean it, maintain it, or organize it. Discover why you desire possessions and choose not to acquire them—this way you're independent from the need to possess. Independence from clutter is freeing.

July 5—Vertical Space

Maximize your vertical space to capture every useable inch. Install shelves to hold books, decor, and baskets to store items. Double hang your clothes in your closet to double your hanging space. Hang kitchen cabinets all the way to the ceiling to maximize vertical space and put a shelf below to easily access frequently used dishes. The large area on the back of a door is almost always overlooked as a way to claim vertical space. Use an over-the-door shoe organizer to store not just shoes but also toys in a child's room; hats, gloves, and scarves in a hall closet; or even cleaning supplies in a laundry room.

July 6—Under Control

Make a list of the areas of your home and life that are under control and detail what makes them under control. Next, list the areas in your home and life that are out of control and detail what makes them out of control. Once you know your strengths and weaknesses, you can leverage your strengths to bring your weaknesses under control. It will take work but don't be afraid to reach out for help to bring your home and life under control. Find a professional organizer in your area to help you organize your home or find a cleaning service or a dog walking service to make life easier so you can focus your time and attention on more important things.

July 7—Tidy

A neat and tidy home can bring great joy to all inhabitants. Take time to tidy. Keep your home tidy by daily maintenance. A little tidying as you go about your day maintains your organizational systems with minimal effort. Tidy up before bed, tidy up before leaving the house. When you tidy here and there, tidying does not become a chore. When you keep a tidy home, you may never again dread unexpected visitors.

July 8—Welcome

Declutter common areas to make your home a welcome place for your family and visitors. Clear some space in the hall closet for your visitors to hang up their coats. Have a bench in the entryway for people to easily remove their shoes. Remove clutter from behind your door so it opens fully to welcome people into your home. Once visitors step through your entryway and enter into your home, treat them to an uncluttered home. As part of your tidying routine, clear off chairs, couches, and tables to give visitors a place to sit or have a meal. A clutter-free home is welcoming to all.

July 9—Visitors

Make out-of-town visitors feel welcome in your home by providing them with little comforts. Stock their bathroom with travel-sized toiletries in case they've forgotten theirs or have run out of anything. Place clean, fluffy towels on the towel rack and remove extraneous items to create a Zen, spa-like experience for your visitor. Change the sheets on their bed and provide an extra pillow or blanket. In the morning, prepare a tray with mugs, sugar, creamer, and a coffee maker or teakettle with a variety of teas. These thoughtful little touches make your visitor feel cared for and welcome in your home.

July 10—Yard Sale

Make some money off your stuff shoved in the back of your closet, up in the attic, down in the basement, or out in the garage and have a yard sale. Set aside items throughout the year in preparation for the sale. Advertise in your local paper, online, and on yard sale apps. Create a large, neon sign that advertises your *Yard Sale!* with your address at the bottom and a large arrow pointing toward your house. Have change—in dollar bills and quarters—on hand to change customers' larger bills. Price all your items to sell and set out housewares on tables and hang clothing on a clothes rack or a clothesline. When your yard sale is over, pack everything that remains into your car and drive it to your nearest donation center. Don't let any items you've already begun to part with come back into your home after your successful yard sale.

July 11—Shred

Paperwork requires only three actions: act on it, file it, or shred/recycle it. If you don't know whether you should shred a piece of paper or recycle it, ask "What would happen if someone got ahold of this information?" Shred anything with your social security number, date of birth, signature, account number, financial information, or credit card information. Invest in a small, crosscut tabletop shredder or a stamp that conceals important information. If you have a lot of shredding, some office supply or package stores charge to shred by the pound. Some neighborhoods even hold shredding events where you bring boxes of paperwork to shred. Don't let your shredding pile up, shred at the end of a paperwork filing session, because if you don't act on it or file it, you can shred it.

July 12—Sale

An item isn't a bargain if you don't have a use for it. When you spend money, any money, on an item you don't need, it's not a bargain. Will Rogers once said, "The quickest way to double your money is to fold it in half and put it in your back pocket." No matter how good the sale is, you're still spending money on something that's going to clutter up your home. This even includes the *buy one get one* at the grocery store. Only pick up as much as you need; most grocery stores offering *buy one get one* will offer just one at half price. Now that's a sale I can get behind.

July 13—Breakup

We've all gone through a breakup at one time, or multiple times, in our life. It's hard to move on and get over the person who broke our heart. We hold on to the memories, both physical and mental, to help us through the pain. But at some point, it's time to clear out the physical memories of the relationship and breakup to move on. Once you've said your goodbye to the relationship and are on your way to healing, trash all the old love letters and mementos and sell or donate the gifts. When you break up with the clutter of the breakup, you're able to move on with your life without the weight of the failed relationship's physical memories bringing you down.

July 14—Attic

For many people, the attic is an underutilized storage space. Organize attic storage into zones, such as seasonal clothing, household decor, and so forth, and label the bins to show what you're storing. Store items in airtight, clear plastic containers. Because of fluctuating temperatures, don't store items sensitive to extreme heat or cold like candles, photographs, or even fine china. Don't store anything in paper boxes as mice and bugs love to chew cardboard and can easily ruin your possessions. If you store seasonal clothing in the attic, be sure to include moth-repellent satchels in the airtight container. By containing and corralling items in the attic, you're able to use this area for all the extra storage it offers.

July 15—Subscriptions

Subscription services are popping up everywhere. In addition to purchasing a subscription for items like magazines or groceries, you can purchase themed subscription boxes. Subscription boxes are like monthly gifts of clutter—which you pay for. Think about that. You pay for a mystery box full of items you don't need and may not even like, and then you do it again the next month. Save the money from a subscription box and ask a friend for a recommendation for a product you may need. Try a sample of the product you want or check the return policy at the store. Cancel your subscriptions, from magazines you don't read to the dreaded subscription box. Your wallet and your home will thank you.

July 16—Purses

Never again be the woman in line fumbling through her purse looking for her wallet or standing in the rain searching for car keys. Organize your purse contents using small mesh pouches with zip closures. Have one for your toiletries (lipstick, hand sanitizer, tissues, gum), one for electronics (headphones, phone charger), and one for other (pen, small paper pad, etc.). When items are no longer running free range along the bottom of your purse or hidden in pockets, you're able to easily pull out and access the pouch you need. Remove any accumulated trash at the end of the day to give your purse a reset.

July 17—Toys

With children come toys—lots and lots of toys. Keep toys organized and in check by limiting the number of toys in your house to only the toys your children actually play with on a regular basis. Sort toys by type—building, figures, and so on—and place them into lidless bins no larger than twelve by twelve inches. Large toy boxes where everything was thrown together and where small toys sink to the bottom are over. Toss broken toys and donate toys in good condition to a local homeless or women's shelter, or check if your local donation center will take toys—many don't. By weeding out the broken and unused toys and containing toys by type, you can keep toys organized in your home. Now teaching children to pick up after themselves is another issue.

July 18—Sell

When you no longer love or need an item, sell it to recoup the cost. In addition to having a yard sale, there are many options to sell your used items—from clothing, to furniture, and even vehicles. Consignment shops are an easy way to make cash on name-brand clothing, shoes, and accessories, or you can sell them yourself online. Collectors scour eBay for vintage or rare items. Craigslist, Facebook Marketplace, and the local classifieds are a great way to sell larger items like furniture or vehicles. Don't let the purchase price of an item you no longer want or need keep it in your life. That's a sunk cost and there are so many ways to sell items to a buyer who will appreciate it—and make you some money.

July 19—Zero In

Know what you want to accomplish out of organizing. Zero in on your priorities by asking yourself what your goal is to better understand your motivation behind the organizing project. Once you understand what you want—for example, an uncluttered living room where your family can gather and play games or watch TV—you can better zero in on a plan of action. When you zero in on the most important reason or area to organize, you can focus your actions with intention. When you zero in on a project, you narrow your focus and can better keep your eye on the goal; you are able to see objectives in an organizing project with laser focus.

July 20—Desire

Every organizing project starts with desire. The desire to find your paperwork when you need it, the desire to make getting dressed in the morning less of a chore, or the desire to have a place for everything and everything in its place. Understand your desires and motivations for organizing to help you make it from the start of a project to its finish. As you feel yourself tiring through the organizing process, think back on why you desired to start the process and hold that goal in mind as you press through to the desired outcome.

July 21—Bins

Everything in your home has a zone, a home, and a container. Plastic bins are great containers to keep items organized. Uniform bins look nicer and more organized than mismatched bins. Match the bin size to the amount of an item you're storing. If you're storing many similar items, subcategorize and place those in a bin. For example, if you have a lot of hair accessories, separate into bobby pins, hair ties, brushes, rollers, and so on until you have a manageable number in a bin. For items stored in a cabinet, use clear plastic bins to easily see the bin's contents without having to read a label. For items in the bathroom or kitchen, plastic can be cleaned in case of a spill. Measure the space before purchasing a bin to ensure you find a perfect match.

July 22—Entryway

The entryway is the first impression visitors have to the interior of your home. Declutter the entryway to make it welcoming. Remove excess shoes from the entryway and store only a few pairs, or none at all, on a shoe rack or shoe mat. Hang keys on small hooks so they have a home and are easily accessible when you leave the house. Hang a mirror to check your look before you head out the door. Install a floating shelf or have a side table by the front door to hold items like your sunglasses and other items that leave the house. If you don't have a coat closet, use hooks or a coat rack to hang coats, hats, and umbrellas. If you don't wear shoes in the house, have a bench where people can sit to remove their shoes. Organizing the entryway makes your home clutter free and welcoming.

July 23—Coins/Change

Coins are currency; we can't just throw them out. But what do we do with them? If you have a change pouch, put the coins in it and leave them in your wallet. That way you'll have change when you are shopping and eliminate the need for a coin jar at home. If you don't have a change pouch, have a coin jar in the entryway of your home and empty your pockets right when you step in the door. When the jar fills up, take it to a counting machine and exchange the coins for bills. Managing your coins may be a change of behavior, but it's a change that pays off. The best way to deal with change is to toss it in the tip jar at your local coffee shop or put it in your change pouch to spend later.

July 24—Junk

The saying goes, "One man's trash is another man's treasure." But what do you do with the things you deem as junk? Sell your junk. Donate your junk. Put your junk in the trash. Whatever you do, just get rid of your junk. Chances are, someone else will come upon it and treasure it, and you both will be better off. Don't let your junk, junk up your life.

July 25—Clothes

We all should present our best selves to the world, both inwardly and outwardly. Your clothes don't have to be expensive or trendy; just make sure that they're clean and well maintained. Adhere to the care labels for your clothes when laundering or having them dry cleaned. Organize your closet so you can see all your clothes. Donate or use for rags any clothing that's torn, stained, or excessively worn. Donate or sell any clothing that's in good condition but doesn't fit you or that you don't feel good about wearing. Your clothes are an expression of yourself. You should feel good and look good in your clothes.

July 26—Hangers

There's one item that has no place in a well-organized closet. Wire hangers. Wire hangers, the kind from the dry cleaners, cause your clothing to pull on the hanger and become misshapen. Treat your clothes well and hang them on streamlined flocked hangers, or wooden hangers for bulky items like suits and blazers. For men's clothing, use plastic hangers since the flocked hangers catch on the clothes when you put the hanger in. To create a uniform closet, use all the same color hangers. Hang all your clothes facing towards you on the hanger so you can see the front of the outfit. Just changing out the hangers in your closet, without even doing any organizing, will give your closet a fresh look.

July 27—Intuitive

Organizing items in your home should be intuitive. Only you can know what feels right for your life. If you're organizing and something doesn't feel right, keep moving it around until it's right. Tune in to your emotions, and you'll intuitively know whether you want a basket or a bin to corral toys, or whether you opt for shelves or a cabinet in the bathroom. Organizing is a very personal preference; use your intuition to personalize your space.

July 28—Neat

Keep your space neat and tidy and neaten your space each day. If you pass by something that's out of place, take a second to put it right. The word neat means "arranged in an orderly, tidy way." Once you've finished an organizing project, don't forget to neaten as necessary.

July 29—Momentum

You'll find that once your space is organized you have a desire, the momentum, to keep it organized. By neatening/tidying every day, you keep that momentum going and keep clutter at bay. Seeing a beautifully organized space gives you the momentum to maintain it. After accomplishing a challenging organizing project, you may even have the momentum to tackle another challenge you've been putting off. Don't let clutter creep in and eliminate your momentum. Keep it up by daily exercising your neatening muscle. Maintain momentum!

July 30—Living Room

Some people say the kitchen is the heart of the home. I believe the living room is the heart of the home. Keep yours family friendly so that people feel invited to sit and stay a while. If you have children, make sure your space is kid friendly with easy-to-clean fabric or even some child-sized chairs. Cozy blankets and lots of pillows that can be used as extra seating are essential living room items. When not in use, store these linens in a storage ottoman coffee table or attractive basket. You can also use baskets in your entertainment center to corral and hide video game controllers. Contain your remotes in a beautiful tray or in a lidded box to hide the remotes when they're not in use. An organized living room is easier to relax in.

July 31 –Wires

I can't wait for the day when everything is wireless. Until then, we have to use some wire management. Keep wires organized by creating the shortest point from the plug to the item. Plug the item in to a power source and gather any excess wire, securing it with a zip tie. Then place the bundle in a cord hider. To organize multiple cords plugged into an outlet or power strip, use washi tape to label each cord. If you can, run wires through the wall to eliminate visible wires along baseboards or the ceiling. Have a charging station where family members can charge their electronics. Toss cords that don't belong to your current electronics and toss any cords with exposed wires. Store excess wires in clear, labeled boxes in a utility area to keep them handy but out of the way.

August 1—Travel

Organize travel items by packing heavy items, like shoes, at the bottom of your suitcase. Wrap shoes in plastic bags or use shoe bags to keep dirt on your shoes from getting on your clothes. Roll clothing and sort by type so you're not rummaging around your luggage looking for a specific item. Pack an empty laundry bag to fill with dirty clothes during your travels. Once you arrive at your destination, hang your clothing so it has time to de wrinkle. Before you travel, check the hotels where you're staying to see if they provide an iron or hair dryer. If they do, you don't even need to pack these items. Pack light and wear clothing you can easily wash or wear with multiple outfits. Use accessories like scarves or jewelry to change your look.

August 2—Suitcase

Once you've returned from a trip, unpack your suitcase within twenty-four hours. You will never have more motivation to unpack the longer your suitcase sits. Take dirty clothes directly to the laundry and restock your toiletries case. Clean off sand or debris and store your suitcase so it's ready for your next trip. Nest suitcases inside each other to save space and encase the smaller suitcase in a trash bag if you're afraid the wheels will transfer dirt onto the other suitcase. Replace a suitcase with a broken wheel, handle, or rips or tears. Make sure your lock is Transportation Security Administration-approved at www.tsa.gov and review weight guidelines for the airline you're traveling.

August 3—Persevere

Completing an organizing project may take some time. Push through any stagnation to prevent backsliding and persevere in your organizing goals. Realistically look at your organizing project and assess your own energy levels to understand the scope of the project you're undertaking. Will you need one day to accomplish your task? One week? If you don't plan your time correctly, you may burn out, and you won't persevere through your project.

August 4—Keepsakes

Whether you call them keepsakes, mementos, or tchotchkes, we all keep something to remember people or events of our past. Display your keepsakes as you see fit or store them in an archival box or plastic tote. Make sure the box is large enough to hold the items you're storing. Keepsakes can be letters, trophies, or even buttons and magnets. Because keepsakes are usually stored, they rarely include photos, which are meant to be seen. Organize and store your photos in photo albums and display them on a shelf where you and others can view them. Periodically review the keepsakes you're storing. Chances are, as you add new items, some old ones may lose their meaning and can be donated or tossed.

August 5—Books

With e-readers people have fewer physical books. Even though book clutter has reduced, there are still books to organize. Have your personal book library organized like an actual library. Sort books by category—you can even alphabetize by author in the category—and store them on a sturdy bookshelf. If you need more than one bookshelf, separate by category to keep similar books together. Store cookbooks in the kitchen where they're used. Children's books should be stored on a bookshelf in the child's room so they can access them. Donate duplicate books, books you've read and won't read again, or those you haven't read and never will. Libraries take donated books for a book sale or for use in the library.

August 6—Delegate

We all wish for more time in the day. One way to capture more time for yourself is to delegate to others. Don't be afraid of delegating, even if you have to take the time to teach someone the way a task is done. Once they know the way to do it, they can take ownership of that task and free it from your to-do list. Delegating age-appropriate tasks to children is a great way to assign responsibility. Delegate to your partner so they can share the household load with you.

August 7—Archive

There's paperwork we need to keep active, and there's paperwork we can archive but still keep semi accessible. This includes past taxes as well as marriage, divorce, birth, and death certificates. If you own property, you can archive the records related to the purchase and any capital improvements. You'll need the paperwork only if you refinance or sell the property. Take a look at your files to see what you can shred and what you can archive to free up space and visually reduce paper clutter. Store archive files in a plastic file tote in a dry environment. Store marriage, divorce, birth, and death certificates in a fireproof safe and have a copy in the archive file tote.

August 8—Arrive Home Routine

You may have a morning and evening routine, but what about having an *arrive home routine* to help you transition between work and home? Creating this routine could mean changing out of work clothes into casual clothes, removing makeup and letting your hair down, kicking off shoes and slipping into slippers. And it should include things like hanging up your bag or purse, putting keys away, and setting your phone aside to power down from the day. For children, their *arrive home routine* may include hanging up coats and backpacks, putting homework in their homework station to work on later, and refueling with a snack. Find a routine that works for you and your family to transition between the outside world and your home life.

August 9—Dollar Store Hacks

The dollar store has some great products that can be hacked into ingenious organizing products. Place plastic cups in a cleaning caddy and use it as an arts and crafts caddy. An office file sorter keeps purses upright in a closet. A muffin tin makes a great container for small office supplies like paperclips and pushpins. The Dollar Store also has great prices on wire bins and wooden crates to use to hold bulky items in the pantry and keep food off the ground. Mason jars are an attractive way to hold paper muffin cups and maximize vertical space because you can stack a lot of cups in the jar. Plastic bins can organize a chest freezer by creating zones, keeping similar items together and organized. It doesn't take a lot of money to get organized at the Dollar Store.

August 10—Clay Pots

Organize with clay pots by using them to hold art supplies on a counter. Or maximize vertical space and hang them from the wall. In the bathroom, small clay pots can hold Q-tips and cotton balls, and the base can hold a bar of soap. Fill pots with glass beads and have them hold makeup brushes. Have your children decorate one and use it as a change jar by the front door. Clay pots are a unique way to corral and organize small items.

August 11—Outdoors

Your home is your greatest investment; love it inside and out. We spend a lot of time cleaning and organizing the inside of our homes, but clutter outdoors makes a home look sloppy. Clear clutter from your yard by taking outdated play sets and broken lawn ornaments to the dump. Hide away trash bins in the garage or on the side of your home. Pamper your yard by planting flowers, mowing, and mulching. Prune overgrown trees and shrubs. Freshen up any peeling or worn paint and fix broken shutters, doors, and windows. By cleaning up and decluttering the outside of your home, you can welcome your family and friends into your beautifully organized interior.

August 12—Purge

While you can organize without purging, I always recommend purging at least a little. We're always bringing things into the home but rarely purging things out of the home. Start purging easy items like excess plastic bags, old paint cans, outdated papers, and ripped and stained clothing. Once you've purged the easily purgeable items in your home, drill down a level and purge duplicates, unnecessary items, and items that were purchased on a whim but never used. When you purge your home of things you no longer need or want, you free the items you do want in your life to come to the foreground.

August 13—Kitchen

Maximize kitchen space by purging duplicate and never-used appliances and tools. Assign kitchen zones such as utensils, pots and pans, baking, spices, and food. Further separate the food zone into canned goods, snacks, and bulk food. Store rarely used appliances on high shelves or in out-of-the way cabinets. Install a blind corner organizer to access the deep reaches of a corner cabinet. Organize spices by cooking type or alphabetically on a spice shelf or spice riser. If you're low on drawer space, store utensils in a crock on the counter. Contain loose snacks like bars and chips in clear or mesh bins so they're contained but easily accessible. Decant bulk items into uniform containers, label contents, and tape cooking instructions to the side of the container. An organized kitchen makes cooking more enjoyable and puts everything you need at your fingertips.

August 14—Clutter

I mention clutter a lot in this book because it's important to banish clutter to achieve an organized home. Clutter may live hidden away in a cabinet or drawer, or it may live out in the open. Review all the areas of your home where clutter lives and either purge it from your home or organize it. Places where clutter commonly lives include the linen closet, desk drawers, back of closets, attic, basement, and garage. Once you address clutter, it loses its power to overwhelm a space and stop you from achieving your goal to become organized.

August 15—Friends

While good friends will accept you no matter what state of organization your home or life is in, it's always nice to have motivation to become organized. Think of your most organized friend. What do you admire about their organization skills? Are they always able to access documents at a moment's notice? Do they have time management down to a science? Are their cabinets always impeccable? Ask your friend how they keep their life/home so organized and how you can do it too. People love to be recognized for their hard work, and chances are they will share their secret of organizational success with you.

August 16—Playroom

First of all, embrace the fact that kids have and come with *stuff.* And that stuff has to be accessible to them in an area near where the family hangs out. Get kids involved in setting up their playroom and keep them accountable for picking up after themselves. Before organizing toys into storage solutions, declutter the playroom. That way the storage solution will only store what you actually need in the playroom. Rotate toys into and out of play to keep kids interested in the toys available. Put items like paint, markers, and Play-Doh on high shelves so they're only accessible with adult supervision. An organized playroom will give your kids hours of playtime and reduce your stress because it's easily organized.

August 17—Bundle

A bundle is defined as a collection of things held together. Bundling is placing likes with likes. Bundle a set of sheets, storing them in the pillowcase of the set. Bundle bobby pins using a magnetic strip mounted inside a medicine cabinet. Keep hair ties secure in your purse by bundling them using a carabineer. Bundle a set of napkin rings using string to ensure that the set stays together. Use containers to bundle small items to keep them part of a set. Bundle similar items together so you can take stock of what you have, and you can keep it organized.

August 18—Read

We all have a stack of things we want to read—whether it's a newsletter, mail from your child's school, or a book—but we rarely have time to sit down and read it. Take advantage of the time you spend waiting and bring that magazine you've been meaning to read but haven't found the time. Tuck some mailings you want to read and discard into your purse or briefcase before heading out the door in the morning. Keep a book in the car for an unexpected wait. Snatching a few minutes of reading time can make you feel productive and relaxed. Don't squander waiting time—relish it as time to pick up your reading material and take your mind away.

August 19—Quit

Good time management is about knowing what to eliminate (quit) from your schedule. There are times in our life when we want to quit a project or a commitment. Before you quit, find the underlying issue(s) causing these feelings. Would switching the time of a commitment work better for your schedule rather than eliminating it entirely? Do you attempt a project when there isn't time to work on it or when you're exhausted, making quitting appealing? If there are ways you can feel better about the situation by making a change, do it. If not, analyze the pros and cons of quitting before you quit. Don't quit something just because it's hard. But do know when to quit something that's unnecessary or unfulfilling.

August 20—Hectic

I have two young children, four pets, a husband, and a career. I know the meaning of the word hectic. Chances are, if you're reading this, you do too. Life can get hectic. Take a deep breath and tell yourself, "This too shall pass." All too quickly, my children will grow up, pets will cross the rainbow bridge, and my husband and I will be in retirement. Deal with your hectic schedule by deleting or delegating tasks. Manage your time by lumping routine and mindless tasks together, like washing dishes and catching up on television shows. Find ways to streamline household processes like meal planning and laundry. Life is hectic, but before you know it, it will pass.

August 21—Meal Planning

When I was younger, I used to ask my mom, "What's for dinner?" Now I ask myself that, and while I can make or buy almost anything, I never know the answer to "What's for dinner?" Meal planning takes the guesswork out of dinner, and since I've shopped for the ingredients based on the recipe, I know I've got what I need. Meal plan your week and create a grocery list based on the plan. Create some wiggle room in the plan for leftovers and a night off. If you're cooking after work, make sure the recipes are easy and don't take a long time to prepare and cook. When your week's meals are planned and easy to prepare, you reduce the need to order out, get takeout, or eat cereal for dinner.

August 22—Collection

We all collect things, almost anything you can think of is collected. Whatever you collect, display it proudly. If you collect books, have a wall of bookshelves organized by subject or author. If you collect dolls, store them in lit curio cabinets where you can see them every day. Hang your painting collection so visitors can admire it. If you collect clothing, build out your closet with enough shelves to store your sweaters or jeans and display your shoes and purses. Keep your collection clean and tidy. A collection in a jumble isn't a collection but quickly becomes junk, collecting dirt and dust and deteriorating. Collections should be organized, exhibited, prized, and displayed.

August 23—Achieve

Achieve your best self by only having items around you that make you happy. Achieve your organizing goal, or any other goal, by starting today. Don't let another day pass without achieving at least one small goal, whether it's drinking eight glasses of water a day or taking the stairs at work. Achieve small goals each day to lead to large results. Even if you don't achieve your goal today, try again tomorrow.

August 24—Bedroom

An organized bedroom helps you sleep better. Remove anything in your room that doesn't belong, and don't bring your computer into the bedroom. Clear the clutter from all surfaces. Banish the chair or exercise equipment that collects dirty clothes, and put dirty clothes directly into the laundry basket. Invest in white sheets to create a clean, airy feel in your bedroom. Open your windows and turn on the fan to ventilate the room. Remove everything from under the bed or only store clean linens or out-of-season clothing in breathable, cotton storage bags. The bedroom is the most important room to organize. You will reap the benefits of an organized bedroom as soon as tonight.

August 25—Baskets

Everything has to have a zone, a home, and a container. While bins are more utilitarian, baskets are an attractive way to corral loose items to keep them better organized. If you're lifting a basket to a shelf over your head, use a lightweight fabric basket and make sure it's not too large. Make sure your basket matches the size of the item you're storing. Don't choose one that's too large or too small to hold everything. From small lidded baskets, to large open baskets, whatever you need to store, there's a basket to store it.

August 26—Computers

Even computers need organizing. We're becoming a paperless society, but just like physical desks, your computer desktop can now become crowded with files. Create folders on your computer to store the files, just as you would a physical filing cabinet. Put frequently used folders on your desktop or within a few access clicks. Put your trash on a schedule to empty itself every thirty days. Use a uniform labeling system for files, either natural caps (Natural Caps) or all caps (ALL CAPS). Periodically go through your files to delete items you no longer need, such as old files and document drafts. An organized computer allows you to easily access files in a few clicks and isn't overloaded with outdated or extraneous information.

August 27—Email

Getting an email inbox to zero is a goal for some people, and I've even heard of a few who have succeeded. Instead of having zero emails in your inbox, use your inbox as a place for current emails you need to address. To eliminate a large amount of email in your inbox, create project or client folders to file correspondence related to a client or a project. When you need to refer back to work done with a client, look in their client folder. When you need to look back on a project, go to the specific project folder. This way your inbox is not cluttered with messages you've addressed, and messages are collated together for future reference. Getting a handle on your inbox makes you more productive, and you will lose fewer emails.

August 28—Sports Equipment

Create a zone where sports equipment lives, usually in the garage, and assign homes and containerize items. I like to store balls and bats in a ball bin and hang tennis rackets on hooks. Helmets can hang on a hook or over the handlebars of a bicycle or scooter. Kneepads and other accessories can live in a bin, making them easily accessible to cushion children's falls. An alternative to a ball bin would be mounting a claw like clip to the wall and each claw holds a large ball like a basketball or soccer ball. There are countless ways to store sports equipment, but always assign a zone where it all lives, and create homes and containerize items.

August 29—Keys

How many times have you misplaced your keys? If you've lost count, this section is for you. To keep a handle on your keys, place them on a hook or on a tray right when you walk in the door. This way they're always by the door when you walk out. Have a separate hook for each person who lives in the house, so they can hang their keys. If you have a hard time keeping track of which keys go to what, color code them by painting the key head with nail polish. Get rid of extraneous keys and fobs. Use your phone number for loyalty rewards instead of swiping a key fob card. Streamlining your keys and installing a key hook is one of the easiest and most timesaving organizing projects you can do.

August 30—Stains

Whenever I'm assessing clothing to get rid of from my closet, anything that's stained has to go. If I really like the item, I will try to get the stain out; otherwise, I put it in donation for fabric recycling. This goes for stained linens as well. Excessively stained napkins and tablecloths are unappetizing. Stained towels are unpleasant. Stained bed-sheets are unsightly. Let stains be an easy way for you to let go of things that are subpar.

August 31—Charging Station

Have a charging station for your family's electronics in a central location, usually a countertop in the kitchen. Stock it with cords for the various electronics and make sure the cords don't leave the charging station. To create your own charging station, use a breadbox as the station so you can close the lid on the electronics. Mount a surge protector strip inside the breadbox—you will need to cut a hole in the back of the box for the cord—and place all electronics chargers on the surge protector. Tie the cords so they're short enough to fit in the space but long enough to charge the electronic. There are also multiple options to buy a charging station as well. Whichever you choose, make sure your home has an area where your electronics can recharge.

September 1—Spices

Whether you cook or barely set foot in the kitchen, you're bound to have some spices that need organizing. You can organize them alphabetically or by type—for example, baking spices, Italian spices, Indian spices. Use shelf risers to give your spices stadium seating or install spice racks on the interior cabinet door. If you have the drawer space, store spices in a drawer. This makes it easy to see the spices you have all at once since they're laid out horizontally. You can also decant spices into uniform containers. Just label the contents and an expiration date.

September 2—Remotes

Remotes make life easier; you don't have to get up to change the TV channel, CD player, or fan. But if your remote is lost, it's of no use. Keep TV remotes near the TV, in a basket or tray, for easy access. Velcro tape air conditioner remotes to the side of the air conditioner. When not in use, the remote can stick to the unit and always be available when needed. Recycle remotes to old electronics. This small act reduces clutter because old remotes are useless. If you're storing an electronic, remove the batteries from the remote to avoid corrosion.

September 3—What If

I used to keep things for the "What if I need it?" times. And you know what? Those times never came. I'd have empty photo frames that I'd purchased without a use because I was afraid that I'd need a picture frame in the future and wouldn't be able to quickly go and procure one. I was cluttering my present for a *what if* in the future. Live in the present and unclutter your home by getting rid of the *what if* items you're holding onto just in case.

September 4—Bathroom

There's never enough room in the bathroom, as it's the smallest room in the house. Create more space by installing a sink with storage drawers. Hang a medicine cabinet that opens to store small daily toiletries. Maximize vertical space by hanging two towel rods on the back of the door, one high and one low. Clear the sink counter to eliminate grime accumulation. If you store cleaning supplies under the bathroom sink, move them to another location to capture all that real estate for toiletries and containerize items in plastic bins by use or type. Use shelves to hold daily supplies and decant items like cotton swabs and cotton balls into pretty containers. Lastly, keep your toothbrush cleared away in a cabinet or drawer.

September 5—ADHD

Attention deficit hyperactivity disorder (ADHD) makes it harder to focus on tasks. If you have ADHD, clear clutter from your workspace to clear your mind and increase concentration. Before you start working, prioritize tasks on paper. Once you're working, focus on one task for a period of time. Don't switch your focus back and forth to multiple projects. Even for people without ADHD, multitasking isn't productive. Manage time using a timer to keep focused on a task. In your daily life, create routines you enact throughout the day, such as a routine for waking and going to bed and a routine for when you come home. These scripts give you control over your time, and the routine acts as a calming mechanism for an overactive mind.

September 6—Command Center

Set up a home command center using a magnetic whiteboard calendar. Record everyone's schedule and activities using different colored markers for each family member. Use magnets to pin up items like a grocery list, permission slips, or tickets. Place the command center in a highly traveled area of the home, like the kitchen, where everyone can review and add to the board. By keeping the family apprised of each member's schedules, you can organize life without forgetting an important event. Customize your command center for your family by including mail slots for each member where you can place their mail for easy retrieval. And remember, with any calendar, it only works if you use it. Get your family on board with writing down their appointments and events so nobody is left out.

September 7—Hoarding

Wikipedia defines compulsive hoarding as a pattern of behavior characterized by excessive acquisition and an inability or unwillingness to discard large quantities of objects that cause significant distress or impairment. Hoarding disorder does not operate in a vacuum but impacts the family and friends of the hoarder. But there is hope for those who hoard. Hoarding is a mental disorder and should be treated through counseling. Identify the need to hoard, resist the urge to acquire, and declutter the home, categorizing possessions and keeping only the essentials. Above all else, treat those who hoard with care and compassion.

September 8—Landing Zone

When you step in the door and put down your keys and bags, this area is called the landing zone. It's the place you *land* first when you walk in the door. An organized landing zone has hooks for your keys, a closet for your coat and hat, and a small trash can for you to empty your pockets and discard junk mail. From there you can distribute mail in the command center. Liven up the landing zone with a cheery mat, sturdy shoe rack, and a comfortable bench or chair for removing and putting on shoes. Your landing zone helps welcome you and your guests into your home.

September 9—Shoes

Shoes take a beating and are one of the wardrobe items frequently in need of replacement. Toss shoes that have holes in them. Donate shoes that don't fit right on your foot or those you loathe to wear. Workout shoes have a life span; I recommend replacing them yearly if you go to the gym a few times a week. You should also have more than one pair of workout shoes to give one a rest if you're a gym rat. If you must hold onto a pair of shoes that's *seen better days*, take it to the cobbler and have the soles replaced or fix any other defects. Present your best self to the world, from your head down to the soles of your shoes.

September 10—Perfection

You may try to be perfect, but chances are, it rarely happens. Give perfection a rest, especially if it's causing stress in other areas of your life. If you're exhausted after a day's work, leave the dishes in the sink. They will still be there tomorrow. Not all homes can be perfect, and that's ok. I tell my clients that the beautiful homes photographed in magazines are staged and cleaned and neatened up right before the photos are taken. If you go to your friend's house and it's always *perfect*, ask yourself if that's even possible in your life. Your friend doesn't have the same circumstances that you do. Strive for what's possible for you, not the perfection you see in glossy magazines or over at the Joneses'.

September 11—Pets

Sometimes I don't know which makes more mess—pets or kids. They both make a mess when they eat, leave toys all over the house, and track mud onto the carpet. Keep pets organized by storing their toys in a bin they can easily access. Contain grooming supplies together so you can grab the nail clippers and the shampoo when you give the dog a bath. Clean out food and water bowls regularly and keep food stored in airtight containers in the pantry. Pet mess cleaning supplies should be kept with the household cleaning supplies. Keep leashes and doggie bags near the front door and hang the leash back up after every walk.

September 12—Linen Closet

Group similar items together and label shelves to keep the linen closet organized. Infrequent items like guest linens or extra blankets can be stored on a higher shelf. Label the shelf so you know what's on it. Store towels together and group them from largest to smallest—body towels, hand towels, washcloths. Store bed linens in a complete set and label the shelf with the sheet's size—king, queen, full/double, twin. Tuck scented sachets or a dryer sheet between the sheets you're storing to keep them smelling fresh.

September 13—Toiletries

Group extra toiletries by type and corral them in clear plastic bins that can easily be wiped down if anything spills. Label the bin for easy retrieval. Place bins on a shelf, creating zones. Hair products go next to the hairdryer and hot rollers. Bandages go next to first aid and medication. Travel toiletries go next to the small travel bags. You can store extra toiletries in the linen closet or in the bathroom cabinet, depending on your space and the number of toiletries you're storing. As always, toss anything you won't use or that is expired.

September 14—Preparation

Prepare yourself for the day ahead by writing out your schedule the night before or early in the morning as part of your daily routine. Lay out your clothing the night before so you can quickly grab it and get dressed the next morning. If you're going somewhere new, prepare the route by mapping out directions. You can never be too prepared. Prepare your family in case of emergency by having everyone know who to call and where to meet. Memorize emergency phone numbers. Prepare for a big test or big meeting as soon as you know it's going to happen. Work backward to schedule what you need to complete before the event. Proper preparation can help prevent catastrophe.

September 15—Under Cabinet

We rarely think of under the kitchen cabinets as useable storage space. However, so many things can be mounted under the cabinets to free up precious counter space. These things include paper towel holders, microwaves, recipe holders, knife blocks, and spice racks. Install a narrow open shelf under the cabinet or a bar to hang baskets or utensils from. Quickly increase space in this underutilized area with a few hooks and hang coffee mugs. Claim the vertical space in your kitchen under your cabinets.

September 16—System

Create systems to better organize your life. A system is a way of doing things, defined as "a set of principles or procedures according to which something is done; an organized scheme or method." When you know how something is done, it removes the guesswork and allows you to focus your concentration on other, more important things. Set up a system for opening the mail and paying bills, doing laundry, emptying the dishwasher, and countless other mundane tasks. Once you create a system for how a task will work, you become more efficient and focused on the task.

September 17—Revise

When you revise your organizing system, you're changing the way it used to work to revise it for the way your life is now. A revision of an organizing system happens when kids grow and their toys change, and you need to redo their room and create new organizational systems for the way they live now. Revising takes the basic framework of your organizing system and tweaks it to work for your life now. You may revise your living room after you get new furniture or revise your closet when you seasonal switch. Revising an organizational system creates large tweaks based on current situations.

September 18—Corner Cabinet

To keep a corner cabinet organized, install a lazy Susan or corner cabinet organizer that pulls out, so items can be easily accessed instead of getting stuck in the back corner. Make the whole cabinet accessible by connecting the two doors together so they open as one. Install lighting in the corner cabinet to illuminate the space. Use baskets to corral items so they don't get lost in the corner and are easy to pull out, or use the space for bulky items. Corner cabinets can be tricky but, when properly organized, can capture a lot of cabinet space.

September 19—Seasonal Switch

A seasonal switch stores out-of-season clothing and replaces it with in-season clothing. If you're storing clothing in the attic or basement, pack clothing in clear plastic bins to keep out pests. Clean clothing before storing as moths are drawn to clothing with sweat or food particles. Tuck lavender sachets between layers of clothing to keep moths away. Fold sweaters when storing; you don't want them to become misshapen on a hanger. Whenever you switch seasons, look at what you're putting away and ask yourself if you wore it that season. If you bypassed it multiple times, it's time to let it go. Recycle any clothing that's excessively worn, torn, or stained.

September 20—Refresh

Every once in a while, your home needs a refresh. A refresh is a simple touch-up of an organizing system, such as matching socks in a drawer or recolor-coding clothing. It's a little more than tidying up but a lot less than creating or rethinking organizing systems. By refreshing your organizing system, you're keeping it going for the long run.

September 21—Sort

Sorting is the second part of my five-part organizing system. Assemble, sort, assess, purge, and organize. When beginning an organizing project, sort all your assembled items into categories to better assess them. Sort likes with likes to see how many of one type of thing you have. You can't assess what you own without sorting similar items together to view them as a whole. When you organize your closet and sort all black shirts together, you can see how many you have and then be able to purge the pile. Sorting also helps you know the size container you need to corral all similar items, which will also determine where you will eventually store them.

September 22—Tools

It doesn't matter whether you're a man or a woman, everyone should have a toolbox. Your toolbox should be small enough to carry around but large enough to fit your frequent around-the-house tools. Fill it with a hammer, screwdriver, wrench, nails and screws, and other items you use around the house. Use small, snack-size plastic bags to contain opened packets of nails and screws or other small items. Separate into multiple bags if storing more than one item. By corralling your tools in a handy toolbox, you'll at least look like you know what you're doing even if you can't actually fix a thing.

September 23—Toxic

Something toxic is extremely harsh, malicious, or harmful. Clutter can be toxic. In a figurative sense—clogging up your life—and in a literal sense, mold and dust mites and vermin (eek!) love to live in clutter. Don't let your possessions become clutter, which can become toxic to the mental and physical health of yourself and your family. Thoroughly clean anything with mold—or better yet, throw it out. Properly store items to keep out vermin and dust. Take care of the possessions that make you happy, and they won't become toxic.

September 24—Credit Score

Check your credit score quarterly to see how it's improving and know what impacts your score. While open credit accounts are important to build your credit score, too many open accounts can hurt it, and destroying a credit card doesn't mean you've closed the account. Call the card issuer or cancel the account online to close it on your credit report. You want to show a long credit history, so keep active any cards you've had for a while. Keep on top of due dates because late payments reflect on your credit score. Sign up for automatic minimum monthly payments in case a payment slips your mind. The more you know about your credit score and the things that affect it, the better off yours will be.

September 25—Paper Management

No matter how minimalist you are, you have some paperwork to manage. Vital documents (birth, death, and marriage certificates) should be stored in a fireproof box. Organize your paperwork in a filing system with hanging and manila folders. Label the hanging folders with broad categories (taxes) and label manila folders with more detailed descriptions (2020 taxes). Once you've created your filing system, it's easy to maintain by filing your paperwork once a week and reviewing to shred outdated documents once a year. Go paperless to reduce the amount of paper you have to manage, and manage the paperwork you need to store in a filing system with hanging and manila folders.

September 26—Try

Oftentimes I combat clients' excuses against trying something new. Sometimes it's object placement in a kitchen, time-management changes, or paradigm shifts to lifestyle. Do yourself a favor and try something new at least once. If it doesn't work for you, you don't have to adopt it. But at least you've tried it, and you know the outcome. You never know how good something can be if you don't try. If you're afraid to start an organizing project, try it out by starting small. Organize a kitchen drawer. See where that progress takes you. Try writing a schedule to better manage your time. Try bringing a bagful of clothing to a local shelter. Try something out of your comfort zone. Try something new. It doesn't matter what you do; just try it!

September 27—Time Management

If only we had more time in the day. A big challenge of time management isn't necessarily having more time; it's managing the time you do have. Prioritize what's important so those items get done. For other tasks, eliminate nonessentials, delegate to others, and hire someone else to do it. You may do some or all of those things to take control of your time. Remember, it's your time; you are in control of it. And you can work better if you manage your time instead of having it manage you.

September 28—Schedule

Time management relies on an organized schedule. Develop a personalized schedule by mapping out your day. Schedule your day in half-hour increments from when you wake up in the morning to when you go to bed at night. Schedule in time to commute, shower, and eat. Add the most important items to your schedule first. These are the things we *have* to do. Carve out time for yourself too; schedule *me time* to feel balanced. Once your day is scheduled, it's easy to run on autopilot because you know where you should be and what you should be doing. If you have a cancellation in your schedule, pull out your to-do list and start working on it. A schedule will make you more productive and focused and certainly more organized.

September 29—X-Ray Vision

We've all done it. Someone's coming over, and you take all the clutter in your home and shove it in an out-of-the way area where nobody will see. And it usually sits there, forgotten. Just because you can't see it doesn't mean that clutter isn't there. Look around your home and pretend that you have X-ray vision. With X-ray vision you can see all those cluttered areas behind closed doors and under beds and in the back of closets. Clear out the clutter and fight the urge to only clear clutter away to where you can't see it. Your X-ray vision can see everything.

September 30—Bills

Few things are more time-sensitive than bills. Keep them organized by setting up a bill-paying schedule where you sit down twice a month—I recommend the Sunday after payday—and send in checks or submit payments. Use a spreadsheet to track the bills, due dates, and payments and balances. When bills come into the house, have a set place to put them. Whether this is an inbox on your desk or an action items folder in your filing cabinet, make sure they are all in one place, so you don't misplace them. Keeping bills organized and setting up a bill-paying schedule will improve your credit score and save money on late fees and interest.

October 1—Checklist

I love lists. Sometimes I'll have a checklist, complete something that wasn't on the list, and put it on the list just to check it off. We have so much to keep track of that lists are important to maintain sanity and accomplish tasks. Checklists are also a good representation of progress. It's very satisfying to look at a to-do list and see most of it crossed off. Daydesigner.com has a variety of free, printable lists to keep you organized. Try out different lists to see if you prefer one running list or multiple lists broken up by project or theme—work projects, home projects, kids. I prefer pen and paper lists, but there are a variety of apps, such as Evernote, that help you keep a checklist, complete with the satisfying check once an item is complete.

October 2—Commitments

Even though you've committed, it's ok to back out of commitments, sometimes. Let whomever you've committed to honestly know why you can't take on another task or commit to another outing. Chances are, they will understand and appreciate that you approached them openly and honestly about your commitments and inability to increase them. You can even say no to commitments at work. Let your boss know what you're working on that takes precedence and offer to help find someone who can take on the new project. When you can't get out of a commitment, refer to your schedule to see where you can make up the time. A well-made schedule has wiggle room for unforeseen commitments without disorganizing the whole schedule.

October 3—Jewelry

Options for storing and organizing jewelry are as varied as the jewelry itself. Some may be as simple as a single jewelry box on a dresser while others are as elaborate as a freestanding jewelry chest. Whatever you choose, hang or place fragile necklaces with thin chains individually to prevent tangling. Stand chunky bracelets up so their side is viewable, and you can see them to select them. Don't store jewelry in the boxes they came in. You can't see the pieces inside, and the boxes aren't uniform enough to stack nicely. Toss them for any jewelry that's not real. If it's for real jewelry, store the box in your fireproof safe. Insure valuable pieces on a jewelry policy or include them with a renter's or homeowner's insurance policy.

October 4—Energy

Understand your circadian rhythm, which, according to the National Sleep Foundation, is basically a twenty-four-hour internal clock running in the background of your brain and cycles between sleepiness and alertness at regular intervals. It's also known as your sleep/wake cycle. Once you know this, you'll know when you will have the energy to tackle a project. Work with your energy cycle to plan your day for maximum efficiency. Being a night owl or a morning person really is a thing! Don't work against your personal energy patterns. Understand and work with your energy to be more productive.

October 5—Car

Our car isn't just for transportation; we eat in it, hold meetings in it, and may even watch movies in it. With all the roles a car plays in such a small space, it's important to keep it clean. A little trash in a car takes up a lot of space. Make it a habit to remove trash from the car every evening. Store plastic bags in the glove box to easily pick up trash. To make car cleanup even easier on you, make this a chore for an older child. Wash and vacuum your car at least every few months—more in the winter because salt from the roads eats car paint. A car free of clutter may save your life. Literally. Clutter can roll under your pedals and cause an accident.

October 6—Lifestyle

Your level of organizing depends a lot on your lifestyle. If you work and have a very active household with kids in after-school activities, your time and energy to organize is going to be limited. Not to mention, the amount of maintenance to keep your home organized will increase. However, hope is not lost, don't give up on organizing. Just understand your lifestyle before you organize to know the upkeep required to maintain the systems and understand that family organizational levels vary depending on the lifestyle of the family.

October 7—Minimalism

My clients love the idea of minimalism. They also try to practice it, to varying degrees of success. We all need things in our lives; we just don't need *all* the things. Minimalism is as much a physical shedding of possessions as it is a mental change to desire experiences over items and to live fully in the moment. As defined by The Minimalists Joshua Fields Millburn and Ryan Nicodemus, "Minimalism is simply the tool to get rid of all the unnecessary stuff in your life so you can focus on what's important; by removing the excess from our lives, we can focus on these musts, and with the clutter gone, we can focus on living a more meaningful life." Make your life as minimalist as you can to create maximum happiness.

October 8—Marriage

Marriage is a joining together of two people for eternity and two people's stuff as well. When you have the joining of the stuff, you're bound to have duplicates. Easy duplicate weed outs are DVDs, CDs, and books. It gets harder to choose which one to part with when it's a kitchen appliance—is the Ninja or the NurtriBullet the better blender? Then there come the argument-causing items like the shoe and purse collection or the movie poster collection. Marriage is about compromise, give and take. You're bringing two households together and merging decor styles and space. Be kind and respect the attachment your spouse has to items as you both decide what stays and what goes as you begin a life together.

October 9—Divorce

If marriage is the merging of the stuff, divorce is the dividing of the stuff. It's a hard, sad time for everyone involved. I hesitate to write about it because it's so depressing, but being organized in a divorce is helpful, and if the information can help someone, I want to include it. Make things smooth and amicable by collecting asset records and taking a household inventory, including video and photographic proof. Your attorney will ask for an accounting of assets and liabilities, as well as monthly and yearly expenses. Getting this information organized in the early stages of separation, when things can be more amicable, will make it easier when the divorce proceedings begin.

October 10—Death

What's sadder than the topic of divorce? It's the topic of death. However, death is inevitable. Children outlive their parents and are left to deal with the accumulation of a lifetime of memories. When you're clearing a loved one's home after their death, look at the items objectively. Sure, Mom loved her afghans, but do you? Or maybe Dad was a Red Socks fan with the memorabilia to match while you love the Yankees. Keep a representative sample of your loved one's favorite things and gift the others to family members who will treasure them or donate items to people who can use them. You can use the sad event of a death in the family to give new life to your loved one's items, either by displaying and remembering or donating to a new home.

October 11—Baby

Now a happy topic: babies. Before you have a child, people may tell you that you need 1,001 things for the baby. You don't. Reduce the clutter that comes with a baby by choosing furniture that can multitask. A dresser with a changing pad on top of it eliminates the need for a separate changing table. Also, there are a lot of things you can do without, like a baby wipe warmer, bottle warmer, and baby bathrobe, and your baby can easily be entertained with half the toys he has. Babies are already complicated and hard to look after. Don't compound that by having to pick up after and clean useless baby items.

October 12—Music

Electronic formats for music change so frequently. Now we download music to stream to our multiple devices. But we still have CDs and even tapes lying around the house. Digitize all your music and donate the hard copy. If you want to keep your CDs, remove them from their jewel cases and place them in a CD case—Case Logic or similar—that holds multiple CDs in a small footprint. Tastes change over time. Be honest with yourself regarding what you'd really listen to. Don't bother digitizing or saving music you would never play. The biggest upside to digitizing your music collection is its accessibility. If you love the music, have it at your fingertips, not sitting on a shelf.

October 13—Goals

We all have goals, and the way we reach them is by working toward our goals every day. My goal was to write this book. And you're reading this because I wrote down incremental steps to accomplish my goal and worked every day (almost) toward it. There's a quote I love that goes, "A little progress each day adds up to big results." It's true that if you do a little toward your goal each day, the goal becomes more attainable. You're also building your goal into a habit, and habits are hard to break. Write your goal down, tell people about it, and have them keep you accountable. And once you've reached your goal, set a new one. You can do it, so start working on your goal today!

October 14—Habit

Habits are involuntary actions—something we are so used to doing that it becomes second nature, like clearing the table after a meal or putting our toothbrush away. There will be roadblocks to good habits, but keep flexing that habit muscle until it's strong. Make it easy to practice your habits. When starting a habit that's different from the way you live, start slow. By starting slow, you are less likely to lose momentum and give up your goal of developing a good habit. It's my habit to clean up the house each evening. Because it's my habit, I don't have to remind myself; I just do it. That's what's great about a habit; you go into autopilot, and it's routine. Habits are hard to break. It's important to make good habits and break bad ones.

October 15—Wardrobe

Organizing your wardrobe starts with purging clothes you no longer want. Your wardrobe is the outward representation of yourself. Rid your closet of anything that doesn't reflect the image you want to convey. Hang as much as you can, so you can easily see your clothes. If choosing outfits in the morning is stressful, group outfits together in your closet or group clothing by type. Store your out-of-season wardrobe so only the items you are currently wearing are in the closet. Update your wardrobe every season and weed out the items that no longer reflect your personality or that are stained, torn, or excessively worn. An up-to-date, organized wardrobe will make getting dressed less of a chore.

October 16—Categorize

I can't think of a single item that doesn't benefit from categorization. Books, papers, clothing, even food are all more organized when they're grouped together in a category. If you're still not sold on the impact of simple categorization, imagine that you're looking for a red pen in a big box of markers, pencils, crayons, and dry-erase markers. It's like looking for a needle in a haystack. Categorizing each type of writing instrument, like pens, into their own section makes retrieval easy. Likewise, searching for a single book among a large collection is overwhelming, but categorizing books by subject or author makes things much easier. Categorization is an easy way to save time and frustration and create a more organized home.

October 17—Social Media

Social media is an essential part of business and personal communication. However, it's important to manage the amount of time spent on social media. In 2017, Mediakix estimated that Americans spend two hours a day on social media. This does not include the other things we do online, like shop and read news. Use timer apps to alert you after a set amount of time on social media. This will rescue you from going down rabbit holes too deeply. Use social media as a reward. Once you've accomplished a small goal, like doing dishes, reward yourself by scrolling down your Twitter feed for a few minutes. Also understand, when lifestyle envy hits, that what's online isn't how people really live; it's just the highlights, with a filter added.

October 18—No

No is so appropriate for so many organizing scenarios. Just say no—to a packed schedule. Just say no—to procrastination. Just say no—to an overflowing closet. Clutter and disorganization don't have to run or ruin your life. Just say no to small things earlier, and small things won't turn into big things. For example, just say no to dropping the mail on the counter without sorting or leaving clothes in a pile on a chair. When you just say no, you stop bad habits from creating a roadblock to organizing success. If your schedule is overwhelming your life and threatening relationships and your sanity, just say no to extraneous commitments. If a commitment doesn't add to your personal, familial, or work goals, just say no.

October 19—Template

A template is a pattern for processes. It's what you use so you don't have to recreate the same steps over and over again. A template can be a preprinted grocery list where you check off what you need. You may use templates at work, where you start a project with an outline that progresses you to the fifth step rather than starting at step one every time. Take any routine steps and create a template. Templates help organize and streamline emails, calendars, lists, and projects. Don't recreate the wheel when you can use a template to make a project or task easier.

October 20—Spend

We spend time, energy, and money purchasing, organizing, cleaning, and in some cases disposing of our possessions. Spend your time, energy, and money wisely. Spend on experiences, not things. Spend time without spending money. Go on a freebie date with the one you love, where you explore your city and check out all the free, local things available. Spend energy on things that add value to your life, like painting your walls a cheery color. Spend money on things that give you time, like a gardener, housekeeper, or an organizer. Spend your precious time, energy, and money wisely, and you won't regret what you spend them on.

October 21—Visualize

I'm sure you've heard it said to visualize what you want in order to achieve your goal. Visualization is important when organizing as well. It helps you develop a vision of how you want your space to look and motivates you toward that goal. When I work with clients, we remove everything from a space to start with a blank slate; it better helps them visualize how they want the finished space to look. Visualize your ideal day, or your ideal desk, or your ideal bedroom, and use that visual to make it happen.

October 22—Pack a Suitcase

Yes, there is a right way to pack a suitcase, and I'm going to tell you how. Pack heavy items, like shoes, on the bottom of the suitcase. Stuff socks in the shoes to save space. Roll clothing to save space, and wear your bulkiest items to avoid having to pack them at all. Seal toiletries double bagged in plastic bags to avoid leaks and place them at the top of the suitcase to avoid crushing. Vacuum seal bags save precious suitcase space. Suitcase cubes keep your clothing sectioned and organized. Choose a mixture of rolling, vacuum bagging, and cubing to organize and pack your suitcase. Bon voyage!

October 23—Pack a Box

When packing for a move, choose sturdy boxes to pack your possessions. Small boxes—nothing much larger than a banker's box, which is twelve by ten by fifteen—are handily sized for heavy items like books. In addition to wrapping a fragile item in bubble wrap or paper, pad the bottom and top of the box to create a cushion for the item. Choose appropriately sized boxes for the items you're packing and fill in any empty space with packing padding to avoid movement or breakage during transport. Use the bottom of wardrobe boxes—the ones with the hanging bar—to transport shoes or bags. No matter how well a box is packed, always remember to label the box contents and room—the room in the new house the box will go to.

October 24—Entertaining

Effortless entertaining requires a lot of effort, and a good host is good at planning and organization. A successful event is planned around the guests. If you use disposable items to entertain, don't store them for next time. Use them up as you would everyday tableware. Chances are, the next time you have a party, there won't be enough of the old, and you'll end up buying new. If you have the room for it, store fine entertaining dishes and linens, and the accompanying candlesticks, vases, and pitchers, in a buffet or server in the dining room. If you don't have the room, store rarely used items on the top shelf of the kitchen cabinets, so they're out of the way of everyday use but still accessible for entertaining.

October 25—Overnight Guests

When hosting overnight guests, set out things your guests would need and enjoy. Give instructions on how to use the television and Wi-Fi. Stock the guest room with an extra blanket, nightlight, bottle of water, and a toothbrush and toothpaste. Sleeping arrangements don't have to be Pinterest-worthy. A clean, cozy, welcoming atmosphere is always best.

October 26—Move

Make moves less stressful by creating a to-do list for the new home and the old home. Choose a mover as soon as you know your move date and check your insurance to see if possessions are insured when they're in transit. Purge broken and unwanted items, so you don't pack, move, and unpack them. Pack an overnight bag with essentials to include a change of clothes, toiletries, toilet paper, paper towels, trash bags, and cleaning wipes. Carry valuables (jewelry, money) with you in case they get lost or stolen in transit. Check garbage and recycling schedules and rules for disposing boxes and packing material. A move is a new beginning. Move only items you want in your life and leave possessions that don't bring you joy.

October 27—Mailing Lists

With e-cards and e-vites, mailing lists may soon become a thing of the past. Until they do, we have to organize them. Start with a spreadsheet of names, addresses, and email addresses. Mail merge—look up directions based on your computer operating system—these contacts into labels and easily print out sticky address labels for invitations, holiday cards, thank-you cards, or "we've moved" cards. Update the list with any returned envelopes. Add columns with phone numbers and birthdays or any other necessary information. Now that addresses are easier to print and you have an updated mailing list, large mailings are much easier and more organized.

October 28—Reduce

Reduce, reuse, and recycle. Maybe you've heard this before from an environmentally friendly friend, or maybe it's your own mantra. Help the environment and your wallet by reducing consumption. Reduce your grocery bill and waste less food by planning meals and shopping for only the ingredients for the meals you plan to make that week. The largest way to reduce is to consume less. Be thoughtful of your purchases and buy quality over quantity. Instead of buying a purse that's on trend that you'll replace in six months, buy a timeless handbag that will last you for years. Manufacturing a product requires raw materials and energy. By reducing the amount of products you purchase, you're reducing your environmental footprint.

October 29—Reuse

The second part of the reduce, reuse, recycle theme is to reuse what you have by repairing it or sharing it with a friend. My sister and I share baby clothes for our children, which we in turn received to reuse from our friends and relatives. Jeans with holes in the knees can become new shorts. Old shirts can be cut up and reused as cleaning rags. Instead of buying new, shop at secondhand stores for household goods and clothing. Reuse what someone else no longer needs to reduce raw material use. Choose reusable utensils, plates, cups, and napkins over disposable at your next party. Reuse what you can to reduce the amount you buy. If you can't reuse, recycle.

October 30—Recycle

Lastly, recycle whatever you can. From newspapers and takeout containers to computers, nearly everything today is recyclable. If you're unsure what to recycle, check out www.epa.gov/recycle. You already know that recycling is beneficial to the environment, but did you also know that recycling creates jobs? A 2016 Environmental Protection Agency study found that a single year of US recycling accounted for 757,000 jobs. You can even recycle expired food by composting at home and using that compost in your garden. By reducing the amount you consume, reusing items, and recycling what you can, you will greatly reduce your environmental footprint and put some money in your pocket.

October 31—Costumes

It's Halloween, the day when children of all ages dress up in costumes that they'll wear once but will clutter your home for years to come. While costumes can have a second life as dress-up clothes, weed out the ones with intricate pieces that a child will never be able to replicate on their own. Donate outgrown costumes and toss costumes with missing parts. If you're short on space, donate large costumes that are difficult to store. Some costumes you may want to save to repeat another year or to pass down to another child. Pack these away with Halloween decorations so you're able to find them next Halloween. Organizing costumes doesn't have to be scary!

November 1—Normal

Every home has a different "normal" amount of clutter. A normal amount of clutter for a single person is not normal for a family of four. You can improve on what's normal and break out of your usual amount of clutter by reducing the number of items in your home. Once you've pared down, create zones for items, assign homes, and containerize to corral clutter. Improve your home's normal through maintenance—putting items away where they belong. This concept of maintenance is similar to how you go regularly to the gym to maintain your fitness. Normal is different from usual. Usual implies complacency. Break out of the usual amount of clutter and get to a normal level for your household based on its size and stage in life.

November 2—Shopping

While we need to shop for necessities, the problem happens when we end up shopping for nonessentials. We've all done it; we've all shopped for clutter. Shopping for clutter is taking a detour down the sale aisle or clicking on a website's "deal of the day." Be mindful when you shop and resist the urge to purchase something that catches your eye. When grocery shopping, stick to the list you made at home, away from impulse buys. Resist the urge to reach out and touch something you didn't come to the store to buy. When shopping online, stay focused on your priorities and don't let your cart fill up with extras. Shop with a purpose and leave the clutter on the store shelf.

November 3—Flat Surfaces

Clear, flat surfaces tend to attract clutter. If you don't know where to put something, and there's a clear flat surface around, chances are you will place it on the flat surface and call it a day. Keep flat surfaces curated with thoughtful decor or devoid of all extraneous items so that something that doesn't belong will stick out. Once one item that doesn't belong lands on a flat surface, others are bound to follow. Know the pitfalls of flat surfaces so you can keep them clutter free.

November 4—Catchall

We all have little items that hang around that we haven't put away yet or things we just don't know where they belong. A small tray can act as a catchall to keep these little items contained until they can be returned to their home or until a home is made for them. Make sure to routinely empty the catchall, as it is just a temporary landing place for items on route to their permanent home.

November 5—Gloves

Winter is coming, and you'll soon be pulling out your winter outerwear. Take a look at your collection of gloves and toss any unmatched pairs or any with holes. Donate any pairs that you won't wear. If you haven't already, wash your gloves before using them this season and store them paired together in a basket or in a clear/mesh over-the-door shoe cubby, one or two pairs per cubby. At the end of the season, reverse the process and wash and match all gloves before storing.

November 6—Alarm Clock

One easy thing to remove from your home is an alarm clock. Most of us sleep with our cell phones on the nightstand or at least in the room with us. Use your cell phone as your alarm clock and get rid of the clunky one sitting atop your nightstand. An alarm clock is just one more item made obsolete by cell phones.

November 7—Belts

Assemble all your belts on the bed to take stock of them. Donate belts that no longer fit or that you no longer like. Toss ones that are broken, either in the belt loop, holes, or buckle. Chances are, you won't fix it, and it will cost more to fix than it will to buy a new one. Once you've got your belt collection down to the ones that fit and that you like, organize belts by type and color. I prefer to have all wide belts together and skinny belts together. Fabric belts would be separated from leather belts and so on. Always hang belts rather than rolling to avoid having them crack or warp over time. Hang belts using the buckle to avoid damaging the material. A belt rack can be easily installed on the side wall of a closet to take up almost no space.

November 8—Need

A *need* and a *want* are very different. Ask yourself before you bring something into your home, "Do I *need* this, or do I *want* this?" A want fuels a desire for a short amount of time. Retail therapy is a momentary monetary distraction from what's really going on in our lives. Be honest with yourself about whether you really need something or whether it's satisfying that fleeting momentary monetary distraction. If you don't address the underlying issue you're trying to distract yourself from through retail therapy, you will continue to want things you don't need and will never satisfy your underlying need.

November 9—Magazines

Start by limiting the number of magazines that come into your home by cancelling subscriptions or moving to online subscriptions. Once you've done this, keep only the current magazine and recycle older issues. If you haven't read it, the information is already outdated and will likely come around again as articles are always refreshed and recycled in a newer issue. Keep magazines in an area where you'll read them. This could be in the bathroom, by your bed, or in the car to quickly grab if you're waiting somewhere. Once you've read a magazine, pass it on to someone else who may enjoy it or drop it in the recycling bin and await the new edition.

November 10—Magazine Holders

In addition to organizing magazines and papers, use magazine holders on their side to keep water bottles from tumbling over in a cabinet. They can also hide electronics like a modem on a shelf. Mount one on the inside of a kitchen cabinet and store cutting boards, Saran Wrap and aluminum foil, or Tupperware lids. For the knitter, magazine racks can hold skeins of yarn. For the gift giver, organize present wrapping supplies using magazine holders, one for bows and ribbon, another for tissue paper. Hang one in the laundry room and keep hangers in it to always have them handy for air-drying clothes. Magazine holders are inexpensive organizing tools with multiple uses.

November 11—Invitations

Gone are the days of everyone sending party invitations by mail. But when you do receive them, what do you do? Always write the date, time, and other important information in your calendar. You can then toss the paper invitation or pin it in the family command center as a physical reminder, for yourself and your family members, of the event. For emailed invitations, put the information in your calendar and file or preferably delete the email. As the date approaches, you are sure to receive additional emailed reminders of the event, and you already have the information in your calendar.

November 12—Identify

Identify your goals and create a plan to achieve them. Identify what you love in your home and eliminate the excess. Identify areas in your schedule that can be tightened up to release pockets of time. Identify possessions and commitments that can be removed from your life. Identify what's working for your household and what's not working and adjust accordingly. Identify and eliminate stressors to make your life happier.

November 13—Clothes Chair

The dreaded clothes chair is one that sits in a corner of the bedroom, and you know it's there but can't see it because it's covered in clothes in varying states of cleanliness.

The clothes chair comes into being when you undress and place clothes on the chair because they're not dirty enough to wash and you're going to wear them again *tomorrow*. Tomorrow comes and goes, and the clothes chair, now established, continues to accumulate more outfits. Remove the clothes chair from the room because it's a useless piece of furniture; otherwise it wouldn't get covered in clothes. This leaves no repository for clothes, so you have to address them, either by tossing them in the laundry or hanging them in the closet to wear again.

November 14—Holidays

The great thing about holidays is that they come about every year. The bad thing about holidays is that they come about every year—and are stressful! Take advantage of this information and plan the holidays out in advance or create running traditions—for example, Thanksgiving at Aunt June's, New Year's Eve hosting a block party with the neighbors. By planning the holidays, down to the menu and guest list, in advance, you're reducing the unknowns and the stress that goes along with it. After each holiday, pack away decor in a labeled box so it's ready for next year. Trade holidays with your relatives, so hosting duties doesn't always fall to you. Don't stress yourself out during the holidays; a little preparation and organization on your part will make the holidays enjoyable.

November 15—Dishes

Even though a set of china as a wedding present isn't a thing anymore, the average household has more dishes

home and not useful for anything but holding knickknacks and collecting dust. Decor on the accent tables change frequently, but as knickknacks are easy to dispose of, accent tables tend to hang around, getting moved from one room to another as the next iteration comes in. Take stock of your accent tables and donate any that aren't used. Keep the ones that are truly useful and let the others go to a home that can use them.

November 25—Boxes

We shop online more than we shop in stores, and countless boxes are delivered to our homes. And it's hard to let go of those good boxes saved *just in case*. So we store them away and keep accumulating. I tell my clients that they will always have a box when they need one. There will always be another box arriving soon. So they can recycle their store of boxes, and nothing bad will happen. This, too, goes for the boxes they're saving *just in case* they move and need to put their stereo system back in its original box. A regular moving box will work just as well, and you won't have to store it for years. If you're not convinced that you won't need your boxes, try getting rid of half of your store. See what happens. Then get rid of all the rest.

November 26—Discard

There's a minimalism game where you discard one thing the first day of the month, two the second, and on and on through the month until you're discarding thirty things on the thirtieth day of the month. What it means is that in a single month you are discarding 465 things—495 if you go to the thirty-first. What could you discard if you really had to? What would add value to your life by removing it from your life? Perhaps the items you discard are digital, like old contacts and photos. Go through your kitchen cabinets and discard expired food. It's easy to find nearly 500 things to discard from your home and life, but you'll never know until you try.

November 27—Food

It's near Thanksgiving in America, and a perfect time to organize your food. Assign zones for food to include breakfast, pasta and rice, snacks, and canned goods. Contain and label smaller items like sauce packets or granola bars in separate plastic bins. Donate food you won't eat and toss expired food. Space on the refrigerator door is good for condiments while milk and juice should live on a shelf for beverages. Separate vegetables and fruits in the large drawers, using the small drawer for lunchmeat and cheese. By creating zones for your food, you reduce buying duplicates. Organizing your food reduces waste because you keep stock of your pantry. An organized refrigerator keeps food from getting lost in the back and becoming a moldy mess.

November 28—Let Go

It's the time of year where we are holding family near and dear, but it's also a great time to let go of some things. Let go of unused or unwanted items. Let go of people and things that clutter up your life. Let go of commitments that clutter your schedule. Let go of preconceived notions of what an *organized* life should be—everyone's viewpoint is different, and the only one that matters is your own. Let go of excuses to become organized; now is always the right time to start. Let go of the past and start living in the present and embrace the future.

November 29—Hair Products

Accumulation of hair products can happen when you buy a product for its promises and are disappointed by the results and search for the next product that offers its own set of usually unfulfilled promises. But what do you do with the nearly full product you've already purchased? Break this cycle by shopping at stores that offer a return if you're not happy with your purchase. Get a sample of the product before committing to the purchase. Or try a product from a friend to make sure it lives up to its promises. Once you've pared your product collection down to only the hair products you use, keep daily hair products in a drawer under the sink or in the shower and infrequent hair products in the linen closet in a bin labeled "hair."

November 30—Blankets

Review your blanket collection to remove the tattered and the itchy blankets. Animal shelters love to receive donated blankets for the dogs and cats. When not in season or use, store clean, bulky blankets on a high shelf in the linen closet or in a canvas bag under the bed. Toss in some cedar and lavender sachets to keep the fabric fresh and moth-free.

For in-use blankets, store them near the extra sheets, so they're easily accessible when changing bed linens.

December 1—Holiday Dishes

Thanksgiving is past, and Christmas and Hanukkah are fast approaching. Each year I unpack holiday decor but never my holiday dishes. Sure, I host dinners and brunches at my home, but I don't use the holiday dishes that well-meaning people gifted upon me over the years. One reason is they're never quite right for my decor, or I'm just not serving the food the dish is made for. Another reason I don't use them is because they are just another item of clutter. If you feel this way about your holiday dishes, pass them on to someone who would enjoy entertaining with or using them. If you don't know anyone you can pass them on to, donate them and have someone come upon them as a treasure. Festive holiday dishes deserve to be able to shine.

December 2—Paint

Have you ever stored cans of paint, thinking they'll still be good when you're ready to use them, only to find out they're an oozy, gooey mess when you're ready to tackle a project? Turns out, there's more to storing paint than leaving them piled up in the garage. Here are some tips to keep paint ready for your next project. Store in an airtight container large enough to fit only the paint, not a lot of air. Label the brand, color, and finish—satin, gloss, semigloss—on the container. You can also write where you painted the color. Store paint at a temperature between sixty and eighty degrees. Now that your paint is properly stored, it will last between three to five years and be organized and ready to use for your next project.

December 3—Sleepwear

Organize sleepwear in a drawer and limit yourself to only the amount that fits comfortably in the drawer. Have three sections: one for sets (keep sets together), one for tops, and one for bottoms. Only keep in-season sleepwear in the drawer; rotate out any seasonal clothes, just as you would with other clothing types. If you only like the top to a set, donate the bottom. There is no rule that says you have to keep matching sets. Only keep what feels comfortable to you. Use the filing system method to fold your sleepwear to keep it upright in the drawer. This way, you are able to see everything you have all at once. You can rest easy now that your sleepwear is organized.

December 4—Puzzles

My mom is a big puzzler. Although she completed scores of puzzles over the years, she never kept them. When I asked her why, she told me the fun was in the making, not in the redoing or the keeping. Completed puzzles were then packed up and donated so someone else could assemble and enjoy. Recycle any puzzles that are missing pieces. Trust me, putting together a puzzle and missing a piece or two at the end is so maddening. For puzzles you do keep, store them in their box or in a bag with the picture of the puzzle so you know what you're putting together.

December 5—Throw Pillows

An easy, inexpensive way to update your decor is to change your throw pillows. Cut down on clutter by keeping the same pillow insert and just changing the throw pillow cover. This way you can have multiple decor options stored in a small space. In addition, edit down the number of throw pillows you set out. Just because something is useful doesn't mean you have to use it.

December 6—Pet Toys

We love our pets and want to spoil them with toys. But just like kids, pets tire of the same toys and need variety. Start to declutter pet toys by tossing broken toys and donating toys your pet no longer enjoys. For the remaining, put away half of the toys and rotate them with the toys that are out. This way you reduce the number of toys while also keeping your pet interested in the toys that they have.

December 7—Pet Food

Assign a zone in your home where pet food will live, ideally near the pet bowls. Keep food in airtight containers, not in the bag it came in from the store. This will reduce the temptation for Fido or Kitty to help themselves and for unwanted pests to snack as well. Use a scoop to easily access the food in the larger container. If you have multiple pets or kinds of food, label each accordingly. For canned food, stack cans with their labels facing out on a shelf near the dry pet food.

December 8—Plastic Utensils

Don't bother storing plastic utensils you bought for a party. When your party is over, use up all the disposable cups, plates, and utensils. Opt out of receiving plastic utensils with takeout food. If you do get them, pack them with kids' lunches or your own for work. If you do store plastic utensils, keep them in the flatware drawer in a separate compartment toward the back or stored in their boxes and bags in the back of the drawer or with entertaining supplies.

December 9—Stockings/Nylons/Pantyhose

Store stockings by type and color in small, labeled bins. I like to label it just what the packaging says—control top sheer and so on. This makes it easier to find the stocking you're looking for without having to put your hands on them and risk a snag to check. Keep stockings snag-free by using a pair of cotton gloves to put the stockings on, eliminating snags from nails or rough skin. Keep a few pairs of new stockings in their package toward the back or side of the drawer and have all others out of packaging for ease of selection and use.

December 10—Nursing

As a mother who nursed, it was important to keep an organized, dedicated nursing drawer for all the accessories and bottles I needed. Have only one type of bottle so parts are interchangeable. Use clear plastic containers to separate bottles, nipples, and pump parts. Corral milk storage bags in a separate container. Store breast pump parts together in their own container as well. Keep similar items together in separate bins in a dedicated nursing drawer or cabinet, so you're not hunting through a large mess of bottle parts when it's feeding time.

December 11—Coupons

Keep coupons in your wallet—since it's a form of money— in your car, or on the refrigerator. Coupons stored out of sight are out of mind and are never used. Periodically review your coupons before shopping and toss expired ones or ones you know you'll never use. You can also use apps like SnipSnap to save coupons to your phone or Retailmenot.com to get coupons and coupon codes for the places you shop. Organized, accessible coupons increase the odds that you'll use them and save money.

December 12—School Supplies

Keep school supplies organized and accessible to bright, young minds. Line empty folders up in magazine holders and keep pens, pencils, markers, highlighters, and crayons separated in a drawer or on a counter in separate containers organized by type. Make sure there's ample paper for writing homework or practicing drawing. You can use a horizontal file holder and keep blank paper, lined paper, and colored paper in a separate cubby. Keeping school supplies organized and handy helps kids easily access the supplies they need.

December 13—Workout Clothes

Keep all workout clothes together in one drawer, including workout bras. Like sleepwear, organize sets together, and then keep tops together and bottoms together. Separate workout shorts from workout pants. Workout socks can be stored in the drawer with regular socks. You can use the filing system method and fold all workout clothing to stand upright in the drawer. But because workout clothing is slippery, you may prefer to stack workout clothing in the drawer, especially because workout clothing can be more of a commodity-type clothing where it doesn't matter which top or bottom you choose. While I can't say that having an organized workout drawer will make you work out more often, it just might.

December 14—Glue

Whether for arts and crafts, home projects, or as an office supply, we've all got it around our house. And chances are, you've got a few tubes that are dried up and useless. Superglue lasts only a few times at most before it dries up, which is why it's sold in such tiny bottles. Toss any dried or empty glue. Combine the white arts and crafts glue bottles if you've got a few that are nearly empty. Make sure that the glue for home projects is stored with tools and hardware, so it's around where you need it. Keep glue tops clean and closed to preserve the glue that's left.

December 15—Trays

I love to use trays to corral items together and keep them organized. Trays on top of a dresser can hold bottles of perfume. A tray near the television neatly holds remotes. Use a tray in the bathroom to keep toiletries together. Wherever you use a tray, corral only similar items. Don't let trays hold dissimilar items; this will turn the tray into essentially a junk drawer. Use trays as helpful organization tools with an aspect of design.

December 16—Textbooks

Each semester, students turn in their textbooks and move on to other classes. Some of those students keep their textbooks and hold onto them, and they sit on the shelf long after graduation. The thing about textbooks is that the information becomes outdated very quickly. In addition, information can easily be found online. Some colleges even buy back used textbooks, or you can sell them online to recoup some of their cost. Sell or recycle old textbooks, get them off your shelves, and free up that space in your home.

December 17—Velcro Strips

One of my favorite ways to use Velcro strips is to attach remotes to their appliances. This way you never have to go searching for the remote. If it's put back, you'll know it's sticking right where it should be. Strips of Velcro can hang lightweight items like corkboards and pictures. Attach power strips with Velcro to the back of furniture to keep them hidden and out of the way. Stick the hook side of a Velcro strip to the inside of a medicine cabinet. Place the loop side of the strip around makeup brushes. This will keep makeup brushes organized and maximize vertical space.

December 18—Nail Polish

Once a bottle of nail polish is opened, you have two years to use it before the polish starts to thicken and separate. Toss old nail polish that has started to separate; you'll know this has happened when you shake the bottle and the color won't come together again. Also toss colors you tried once but didn't like and polishes that are streaky and don't spread well. Store polish bottles upright in a room-temperature environment away from sunlight. For extra organization, keep them in a container with nail files and clippers to create a manicure-ready set.

December 19—Shelves

Assign zones for your shelves to keep them organized. Whether it's in the kitchen, on a bookshelf, or in the garage, group similar items together on a shelf. By assigning zones to shelves, it helps you remember where things are, and you can keep track of your categories. Keep pasta and rice together on the same shelf, keep all history books together on a bookshelf, and in the garage keep sports equipment together on a shelf. Adjustable shelving is a plus if you have it. Whether it's for toys that change as kids grow or garage items that cycle in and out over the years, being able to adjust the height of a shelf, or even take one out, is a bonus. If you have open shelving, it's even more important to keep it organized and neat.

December 20—Skincare

Keep skincare organized by grouping it together by use. Keep night creams and serums separate from day creams. Masks should be separate from daily use skincare. Once you've separated skincare, store them in the medicine cabinet and corral them in short, clear rectangular containers. These containers will keep skincare products from falling out of the medicine cabinet's narrow shelves. Another option to organize skincare is to use a divided lazy Susan/turntable. Keep it on the counter or in a drawer to stash daily skincare products. No matter the container you use, label the different sections to make it easy to remember where products live.

December 21—Coats

In these chilly winter months—today being the start of winter—we bundle up in our coats to go anywhere. Keep coats organized by always hanging them up when you arrive home. Wet winter coats become musty if left in a pile on the floor or on a chair. Invest in coat hangers for your coat closet to ensure that every coat has a sturdy hanger, to keep the coat hung up, and also help the coat keep its shape. When it's time to pack up coats for the season, clean them in the washer, by spot cleaning, or by dry cleaning. Then, pack them in linen clothing bags with lavender and cedar sachets to keep moths away. Store in the back of the closet or in the attic or basement until next season when you pull out clean, ready-to-wear coats.

December 22—Sewing

Many sewing supplies are small items like buttons, pins, and needles. Keep these small items organized and accessible using a magnetic spice organizer system. These little jars have clear lids and maximize vertical space in a sewing area. If you like your sewing supplies to be portable, use a tackle box or toolbox to store supplies. The large area on the bottom of a toolbox is perfect for fabric, while the smaller divided sections can hold sewing supplies. Use mason jars to organize a supply of buttons near the sewing machine. Another large mason jar can hold spools of thread.

December 23—Towels

Purge your linen closet of stained, torn, or excessively worn towels. Also, get rid of unmatched sets and excess towels. Keep only two sets of towels per person, a wear and a spare. Donate old and extra towels to your local animal shelter. Once your closet is purged of towels, organize by type. Body towels together, hand towels together, washcloths together. Keep all towels in the linen closet or in their corresponding bathroom. You can roll towels and place them upright in a bin, or you can fold them and stack them on a shelf.

December 24—Trunk

An antique trunk offers multiple organizing uses and adds a decorative accent to a room. Use a trunk at the foot of the bed to store linens. Install dividers in the trunk and use it to organize shoes. Store memories in a trunk. Use it as a coffee table and keep games inside. Repurpose it into a bar by installing shelving. Install rods and make a trunk into file storage. Line it with cedar and store seasonal clothing. Using or repurposing a trunk keeps history alive and offers a storage/furniture piece combination.

December 25—Gifts

When shopping for gifts, give experiences not items. Experiences last a lifetime and don't clutter up a person's home. Better yet, give an experience you can enjoy too, like movie tickets or dinner at a nice restaurant. Cash is a gift everyone likes, especially teenagers who enjoy picking out their own gifts or using it to fund a larger purchase like a car or their education. Gift cards are great gifts for coworkers and babysitters. You don't even have to spend money to give someone a gift. Parents love to receive coupon booklets from their children, no matter the age. Give your neighbor the gift of shoveling their sidewalk or bring a plate of cookies. The best gifts are free and come from the heart.

December 26—Return

Take advantage of a return policy if you're unhappy with a product's performance or have any buyer's remorse. I've returned clothing and shoes, toys, and household products that I was unhappy with or purchased but didn't end up needing. Don't let a purchase or gift clutter your life when you can return it and get your money back or get something that you enjoy. If you are returning a product, don't let the return period lapse and leave you with an unwanted item. If you don't have the receipt, many stores can look up the purchase using the credit card you paid with. Alternately, you can exchange for store credit. Whether you receive a refund or store credit, you're better off without the item cluttering your home. If you can't return something, donate or give it as a gift to someone who may want or use it.

December 27—Table Linens

Review table linens and donate linens that are stained or ripped or that don't fit your table—for example, if you have a square tablecloth, but your table is rectangular. Wash and iron any dirty linens. Organize by type, grouping runners together, placemats together, and tablecloths together. Napkins go with their matching set, or separate if they can be used across sets. Fold sets up together and place in a drawer near the table you'll be setting. If you have seasonal linens, store them with seasonal decor, so they're not taking up space year-round with daily table linens.

December 28—Birthdays

Keep a supply of gifts, wrapping supplies, and cards on hand for birthdays. You can re-gift unopened duplicate toys your children receive for when their friends have a birthday. Have a designated place where you keep the gifts and supplies and pull from there should you need a gift. For birthday entertaining, use up all the entertaining supplies after the party. Don't store the extra cups, plates, napkins, and silverware. Chances are, your next party won't be the same theme, or you won't have enough left over to cover a new party. Or use a singular color you can reuse year after year.

December 29—Surfaces

Keep surfaces free of clutter by putting away items that don't belong. It's nearly impossible to make a meal, eat at the dining room table, or work at a desk when the surface is cluttered. Use the vertical wall space to house items rather than having them live on a surface. This frees up the surface to be a workspace. This works well in the garage when tools hang on the wall or live in a cabinet and the surface workspace is clear. The same goes in the kitchen, hanging knives on a magnetic knife holder on the backsplash frees up the counter surface for food preparation. Organized surfaces don't become a catchall for clutter.

December 30—Perfume

Organize perfume by scent and type—all body sprays stored together, floral scents together, woodsy scents, and so on. Keep perfume out of direct sunlight and heat, so don't store by a window or in the bathroom. I prefer to keep perfume on a tray in the closet so you can apply it before dressing. Toss any fragrances that have turned sour and donate any that you no longer like.

December 31—Why

Know why you're organizing before you start organizing. Are you organizing to prepare for a major life change? Are you organizing to reduce clutter from your home and gain control over your possessions? Do you want to manage your time and be proactive rather than reactive? You will be more motivated to push through and accomplish your task when you have a clear reason why you're organizing. Don't organize to go minimalist because that's what everyone's doing. Have your own reasons why and incorporate them into your project goal. If you have a clear goal of why you're undertaking the project, it will help when you're purging things from the past to make way for things for the future.

www.ingramcontent.com/pod-product-compliance
Lightning Source LLC
Chambersburg PA
CBHW071053040426
42443CB00013B/3321